D1575695

WITHDRAWN
FROM THE RECORDS OF THE
MID-CONTINENT PUBLIC LIBRARY

J974.48202 Ed96
Edwards, Judith
The Plymouth Colony and the
 Pilgrim adventure in...

MID-CONTINENT PUBLIC LIBRARY
Raytown Branch
6131 Raytown Road
Raytown, Mo. 64133

RT

THE PLYMOUTH COLONY AND THE PILGRIM ADVENTURE IN AMERICAN HISTORY

The IN AMERICAN HISTORY Series

The African-American Struggle
for Legal Equality
(ISBN 0-7660-1415-0)

The Alaska Purchase
(ISBN 0-7660-1138-0)

Alcatraz Prison
(ISBN 0-89490-990-8)

The Battle of Gettysburg
(ISBN 0-7660-1455-X)

The Bombing of Pearl Harbor
(ISBN 0-7660-1126-7)

The Boston Tea Party
(ISBN 0-7660-1139-9)

Charles Lindbergh and the
Spirit of St. Louis
(ISBN 0-7660-1683-8)

The Chisholm Trail
(ISBN 0-7660-1345-6)

The Confederacy and the Civil War
(ISBN 0-7660-1417-7)

The Cuban Missile Crisis
(ISBN 0-7660-1414-2)

The Dust Bowl and the Depression
(ISBN 0-7660-1838-5)

The Fight for Women's Right to Vote
(ISBN 0-89490-986-X)

The Harlem Renaissance
(ISBN 0-7660-1458-4)

The Home Front During World War II
(ISBN 0-7660-1984-5)

The Industrial Revolution
(ISBN 0-89490-985-1)

Jamestown, John Smith, and Pocahontas
(ISBN 0-7660-1842-3)

The Jim Crow Laws and Racism
(ISBN 0-7660-1297-2)

John Brown's Raid on Harpers Ferry
(ISBN 0-7660-1123-2)

Lewis and Clark's Journey of Discovery
(ISBN 0-7660-1127-5)

Lincoln and the Emancipation
Proclamation
(ISBN 0-7660-1456-8)

The Lincoln Assassination
(ISBN 0-89490-886-3)

The Lindbergh Baby Kidnapping
(ISBN 0-7660-1299-9)

The Little Rock School
Desegregation Crisis
(ISBN 0-7660-1298-0)

The Louisiana Purchase
(ISBN 0-7660-1301-4)

The Manhattan Project
and the Atomic Bomb
(ISBN 0-89490-879-0)

McCarthy and the Fear
of Communism
(ISBN 0-89490-987-8)

The Mission Trails
(ISBN 0-7660-1349-9)

The Mormon Trail
and the Latter-day Saints
(ISBN 0-89490-988-6)

The Natchez Trace Historic Trail
(ISBN 0-7660-1344-8)

Nat Turner's Slave Rebellion
(ISBN 0-7660-1302-2)

The New Deal and the Great Depression
(ISBN 0-7660-1421-5)

The Panama Canal
(ISBN 0-7660-1216-6)

The Pony Express
(ISBN 0-7660-1296-4)

The Prohibition Era
(ISBN 0-7660-1840-7)

The Pullman Strike and
the Labor Movement
(ISBN 0-7660-1300-6)

Reconstruction Following
the Civil War
(ISBN 0-7660-1140-2)

The Salem Witchcraft Trials
(ISBN 0-7660-1125-9)

The Santa Fe Trail
(ISBN 0-7660-1348-0)

Shays' Rebellion and the Constitution
(ISBN 0-7660-1418-5)

Slavery and Abolition
(ISBN 0-7660-1124-0)

The Space Shuttle *Challenger* Disaster
(ISBN 0-7660-1419-3)

The Triangle Shirtwaist Fire and
Sweatshop Reform
(ISBN 0-7660-1839-3)

The Union and the Civil War
(ISBN 0-7660-1416-9)

The Vietnam Antiwar Movement
(ISBN 0-7660-1295-6)

The Watergate Scandal
(ISBN 0-89490-883-9)

Westward Expansion and
Manifest Destiny
(ISBN 0-7660-1457-6)

The Plymouth Colony and the Pilgrim Adventure in American History

Judith Edwards

Enslow Publishers, Inc.

40 Industrial Road   PO Box 38
Box 398   Aldershot
Berkeley Heights, NJ 07922 Hants GU12 6BP
USA   UK

http://www.enslow.com

MID-CONTINENT PUBLIC LIBRARY
Raytown Branch
6131 Raytown Road
Raytown, Mo. 64133

RT

MID-CONTINENT PUBLIC LIBRARY

3 0000 12386232 2

Copyright © 2003 by Judith Edwards

All rights reserved.

No part of this book may be reproduced by any means
without the written permission of the publisher.

Library of Congress Cataloging-in-Publication Data

Edwards, Judith, 1940–
    The Plymouth Colony and the Pilgrim adventure in American history /
Judith Edwards.
        p. cm. — (In American history)
        Summary: Traces the dangers and adventures surrounding the history of
    the Pilgrim settlement at Plymouth, Massachusetts, highlighting the roles
    played by William Brewster, Miles Standish, and other individuals.
        Includes bibliographical references and index.
        ISBN 0-7660-1989-6
        1. Massachusetts—History—New Plymouth, 1620–1691—Juvenile
    literature. 2. Pilgrims (New Plymouth Colony)—Juvenile literature.
    [1. Massachusetts—History—New Plymouth, 1620–1691. 2. Pilgrims
    (New Plymouth Colony)] I. Title. II. Series.
    F68.E25   2003
    974.4'8202—dc21
                                                    2002012809

Printed in the United States of America

10 9 8 7 6 5 4 3 2 1

To Our Readers: We have done our best to make sure all Internet Addresses in this
book were active and appropriate when we went to press. However, the author and
the publisher have no control over and assume no liability for the material available
on those Internet sites or on other Web sites they may link to. Any comments or
suggestions can be sent by e-mail to comments@enslow.com or to the address on
the back cover.

Illustration Credits: Enslow Publishers, Inc., pp. 6, 15, 25, 32, 44,
114; Judith Edwards, pp. 36, 42, 54, 67, 75, 79, 87, 92, 103, 106, 108,
111; Reproduced from Charles Hograth's *Illustrations of World-Famous
Places*, Dover Publications, Inc., 1993, p. 18; Reproduced from the
Collections of the Library of Congress, pp. 46, 50, 51, 63, 68, 78, 85,
102, 113; Reproduced from the *Dictionary of American Portraits*
published by Dover Publications, Inc., in 1967, pp. 30, 58.

Cover Illustration: Reproduced from the Collections of the Library of
Congress (Large vertical photo and top and bottom horizontal photos);
Reproduced from the *Dictionary of American Portraits* published by
Dover Publications, Inc., in 1967 (Small vertical photo).

★ CONTENTS ★

1 Land Ho!   7

2 In Search of Religious
    Freedom   11

3 The First Emigration   22

4 Setting Out for America   35

5 The Mayflower Compact   41

6 The Howling of Wolves   53

7 Betrayal and the Threat
    of War   70

8 Hunger, Treachery,
    and Pirates   90

9 Daily Life at Plymouth 101

10 Expansion and Legacy 110

    Timeline 117

    Chapter Notes 120

    Further Reading 124

    Internet Addresses 125

    Index 126

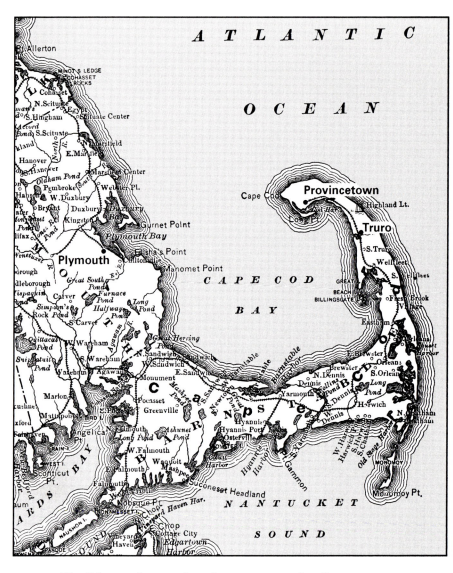

The Pilgrims first anchored near present-day Provincetown. What they would call Corn Hill was near present-day Truro. The Pilgrims finally established a permanent settlement at Plymouth.

"After many difficulties in boisterous storms, at length by God's good providence we espied [saw] land, which by break of the day we deemed to be Cape Cod." So begins an entry in *Mourt's Relation*, the earliest journal of Plymouth plantation.[1] For over two months, 102 people had

LAND HO!

been squeezed onto a ship meant to carry only cargo, when, at dawn on November 9, 1620, land was sighted! After sailing for sixty-six days on the Atlantic Ocean from Plymouth, England, they saw the cliffs of Truro, Cape Cod (in present-day Massachusetts). "The appearance of it much comforted us, especially seeing so goodly a land and wooded to the brink of the sea. It caused us to rejoice together and praise God that had given us once again to see land," describes the unknown writer of *Mourt's Relation*.[2]

On the *Mayflower*

After experiencing some rough water close to shore, the *Mayflower*, a sturdy ship of 180 tons, sailed around the cliffs and entered Provincetown Harbor. Of course, everyone wanted to get off the ship at once.

Most people had slept in the main cabin of the ship, where no one over five feet tall could walk without bending over. The Pilgrims could not wash themselves. Everyone itched from lice and fleas and smelled bad.

Food was barely edible. The cheese had gone moldy, and the mice and rats competed for the dried peas kept in sacks. Hard biscuits were stacked around the ship. Even those had gone stale or been nibbled by little bugs called weevils, as well as maggots and rats. Luckily there were some vegetables such as cabbages and turnips.[3] Meat included dried codfish and ox tongues, and salted pork and beef.

Only one sailor and one Pilgrim had died on the whole trip. However, everyone was weak, incredibly uncomfortable, and ready to put their feet on land. The sailors were tired, too, and disgusted with what they considered to be a bunch of people who were good for nothing but praying. The Pilgrims disliked the sailors' rough language, so the sailors roughened it more. Time to get off this ship!

The problem was, where were they? No welcoming lights from houses appeared on shore. Would they be killed by American Indians as soon as their feet touched land? It was getting close to winter— they needed to find a place to settle. They would have to send exploring parties out, and if the women and children came to shore to do laundry, set up a guard for them.

Above Virginia

The *Mayflower* had actually ended up outside of the territory of the patent that allowed them to set up a colony. The entire English claim in North America was at that time called Virginia. To settle in Virginia, a group had to have legal permission from the king of England.

Two companies administered these claims. One was the Virginia Company of London, which had founded Jamestown in 1607. The other was the Virginia Company of Plymouth. This Virginia Company also sent out an expedition in 1607 but failed to start a colony. Between 1607 and 1618, when the Pilgrims decided to sail for the New World, the Virginia Company of London had expanded northward. In order to attract investors, they set up an idea called "particular plantation," which allowed a group to have a temporary charter that could lead to legal title, after an agreed-upon term, to the land they settled.

The Merchant Adventurers, who had funded the Pilgrims' voyage, had obtained a patent for a particular plantation in 1620. Now the Pilgrims had arrived just north of where the Virginia settlement ended. The term *New England*, which was applied to the northern part of the Virginia claim, would not apply to all of what we now know as New England for another few years.

Saints and Strangers

This confusion was all the worse because there were two distinct groups aboard the *Mayflower*. Forty-six of the Pilgrims on board the *Mayflower* were called Separatists, which meant that they wanted to form a church totally separate from the Church of England. They had gone to Holland to escape persecution for their beliefs. The Separatists called themselves Saints. They called the others, those who followed the Church of England and had come to America for economic reasons, Strangers. The leaders of the Saints insisted that an agreement be signed before anyone left the ship, especially since they had landed outside of the territory of their patent.

A mutiny was brewing, just as this tired, hungry, itchy, sore, and smelly bunch of Pilgrims saw relief across the harbor.

The general definition of the word *pilgrim* is "one who travels to a foreign land, usually to a holy place to pray." Some of these pilgrims who crossed the Atlantic to this new land, sought a place where they could worship God in their own way. They desired the freedom to form their own beliefs and conduct their worship services and their lives the way they wanted.

IN SEARCH OF RELIGIOUS FREEDOM

A Changing World

The passengers of the *Mayflower* lived at a time when there was much change and unrest going on. The world they had left across the ocean had been engaged in religious wars and revolutions for an entire century.

Christianity was founded on the belief that God had a son named Jesus, who died as a sacrifice for the sins of mankind and was resurrected, or reborn, into the kingdom of God. The Christian Roman Catholic Church dominated Western Europe. The pope, whose power Catholics believe comes directly from God, had more power than the rulers of any country. The Church owned one third of all the land in Europe, and it grew very rich during the Middle Ages.

The first important voice of objection to the Church was John Wyclif, a fourteenth-century English priest and scholar. He believed that men should obey only God, and not priests and bishops, whose allegiance was to the pope. Wyclif's belief was that people should be able to read the Bible and decide for themselves about the worship of God. For his beliefs, John Wyclif was persecuted and banned from the priesthood.

Martin Luther also put forth the idea that obeying the priests was not the only path to God's grace. Luther, a German who lived from 1483 to 1546, believed that the Bible is the only teacher necessary. Many important princes in Germany supported Luther. In 1529, the princes were ordered by the pope to return to the Catholic Church. Their protest against this ruling gave us the word *protestant*.

Luther felt that the church structure needed to be reformed. This led to what is known as the Protestant Reformation. Those who followed the teachings of Luther were called Lutherans. By 1536, Norway, Denmark, and Sweden had *only* the Lutheran Church. Wars between the Lutherans and the Catholics erupted and continued until 1648.

In France, John Calvin also spoke out about the importance of obeying the Bible over the priests. He believed in a strict, hardworking, disciplined life as the means of reaching salvation. These values have taken his name, which has come down to us in the term *Calvinism*.

The Dutch embraced the Reformation and started many Protestant churches. Holland, in the sixteenth century, was ruled by Spain and its Catholic ruler, Philip II. In 1567, Philip sent an army to towns where reformed churches had taken hold. He ordered the execution of eighteen thousand Protestant Dutch. In 1648, after eighty years of periodic fighting, Holland won complete freedom to be a Protestant country.

Henry VIII's Big Decision

In England, the Reformation did not really start until King Henry VIII could not, as a Catholic, get his marriage annulled so he could remarry. Since he was used to doing what he wanted, he decided that he would become the head of the Protestant Church of England. He broke with the Catholic Church in 1534.

Bloody Mary

Henry VIII was succeeded by his young son, Edward VI, who was also Protestant. When Edward died, his half sister Mary, a devout Catholic, took the throne. She had the power to return England to the Catholic Church. Bloody Mary, as she came to be known, ruled for five years. Three hundred Protestants were killed by burning at the stake during her reign. Mary's death brought to the throne her half sister Elizabeth.

Elizabeth's Reign

Elizabeth, a Protestant, ruled for forty-five years, from 1558 to 1603. Many of those who sailed on the *Mayflower* were born during the Elizabethan era. Unfortunately, Elizabeth was as rigid about the expression of Protestantism as the bishops were about Catholicism. She wanted no fighting over various ways of holding worship. Everyone would embrace the elaborate rituals of the Church of England; all books printed would be with her permission; and if a person refused to go to church, he or she would be jailed. If one held views that differed from those held by the Church of England, there was a risk of being burned at the stake.

Puritans and Separatists

There were those who wanted to practice Christianity without all the rituals. They believed that only what was mentioned in the Bible should be included in church services, and thought that Christianity should be restored to its "ancient purity." These people were called Puritans.

A student of religion at Cambridge, Robert Browne believed in going several steps beyond reform. His sermons, which got him removed from the university, insisted that the Puritans must separate totally from the Church of England. Those who believed as he did

Many of the Separatists were from the English countryside, where church buildings were very simple.

would form their own congregations, or assemblies of believers, with the church officials coming from within the congregation. Since a license from the queen was needed to preach, this belief in itself helped send Browne to jail.

Those who believed as Browne did came to be called Brownists, or Separatists. After his release, he and his fellow Separatists left for Holland. Though still in the middle of recurring battles with the Catholic Church, Holland was a country where they would be allowed freedom of worship.

Young William Brewster

William Brewster, born in 1567, was the son of the manager of a large estate, called a landholding, owned by the Archbishop of York. There were many villages and farms on this manor, and the senior William Brewster collected rent from these tenants. He eventually became the postmaster at the town of Scrooby and was allowed to live with his family in the manor house.

The young William Brewster learned to read and write and went to Cambridge University at the age of fourteen. The Cambridge of William Brewster's day was not very calm. Browne had stirred up trouble, and among the student body were such radical thinkers as John Penry and John Greenwood.

In 1583, sixteen-year-old William left Cambridge and began working for Sir William Davison, a diplomat trusted by the queen. William was employed as a personal servant and confidential messenger.

Unfortunately for Davison, he was implicated in the 1587 beheading of Mary, Queen of Scots, a Catholic cousin of Queen Elizabeth. Though Elizabeth herself had issued the death warrant, she claimed she really had not wanted it carried through. Davison became a scapegoat, someone who is blamed for actions or mistakes caused by another person. Davison was imprisoned in the Tower of London, where William Brewster still served him. In 1588, the Spanish Armada, a great fleet of ships, attacked the English and Dutch and tried to invade England. The Armada was defeated by the British Navy under the command of Sir Francis Drake. In all the turmoil, Davison managed to escape execution.

Death and Marriage

Brewster was called home from serving Davison in 1589. Brewster's father was ill, and he was needed to take over his post. Brewster left London for a little town that would not welcome his religious views. The elder William Brewster died in 1590, and Sir Samuel Sandys, inheritor of the Scrooby estate, asked twenty-four-year-old William Brewster to stay on as manager and postmaster.

Brewster soon married. Having lived in the world of royalty, he knew about the need to keep his religious views away from the eyes of authority. Conflicts between the Puritans and Separatists on the one hand and the established Church of England on the other continued to grow all around England. Pamphlets were written and secretly circulated in both London and rural villages. These pamphlets, or tracts, made fun of the Church of England's bishops.

Finally, a man who had signed the pamphlets as "Martin Mar-Prelate," was arrested in 1593. This man was John Penry, who had been at Cambridge with Brewster. Penry was hanged, which had been John Greenwood's fate two months earlier.

Six miles from Scrooby, a minister named Richard Clyfton preached reform of the Church to his Babworth congregation. William Brewster and his family attended this church. Other Puritan churches sprang up near Scrooby.

In 1602, Brewster befriended a twelve-year-old boy named William Bradford. Bradford's parents had died when he was very young, and he had lived with his grandfather and then his uncles since he was eight. He was very religious, somewhat sickly, and very interested in church reform.

Queen Elizabeth died in 1603. The new King of England, James I, was even more rigid about Church of England attendance and ritual than Elizabeth had been.

James I Disappoints the Puritans

The Puritans had hoped that James I would be a good reformer, since he had been king of a Presbyterian country—Scotland. They decided to present their wishes for reform. Eight hundred ministers signed the Millenary Petition. They wanted the king to demand that the Sabbath be kept without wild and "profane" festivities.

Originally built for use by the English Catholic Church, Westminster Abbey became a Church of England building after the country's religious conversion. Its expensive, fancy style symbolized much of what the Separatists were trying to break away from.

They wanted the king also to guarantee that the Church of England ministers were actually intelligent, well educated, hard working, and that they would stop wearing ornate robes similar to those of Catholic priests.

The Puritans were laughed at for their stern views, and James I was furious. James refused to include Puritan ministers in important conferences. When four Puritans were finally allowed into a conference at Hampton Court Palace, they asked that the king grant them liberty of conscience—the right to worship God as they wanted to. James knew that the Puritans wanted to elect their own ministers. He believed this weakened his power, and the Divine Right of Kings— the idea that the king's power came directly from God. This was very similar to the Catholic idea that the pope's power came directly from God. According to historian Frank G. Beardsley, James said, "I will have none of that, I will have one doctrine and one discipline, one Religion in substance, and in ceremony."[1]

James would concede nothing that threatened his absolute, or total, rule. He had lived with the Presbyterian Church in Scotland and did not want a similar church in England. He would have bishops chosen by him to rule his church with him. "I will make them (the Puritans) conform, or I will harry [annoy and be unfair to] them out of the land."[2]

Secret Meetings

A period of extreme measures began against both Puritans and Separatists. All religious meetings were forbidden. No book but the English prayer book was to be allowed in churches. Three hundred ministers who refused to follow James's rules were removed from their churches. As it became clear that no reform was possible, Separatist congregations met more and more in secret.

There was already a radical Separatist congregation at Gainsborough, eight miles from Scrooby. In 1606, this congregation divided, and about forty-five people began to meet at Scrooby, under Richard Clyfton. The meetings were secret and were held in the manor house where William Brewster lived.

By now, the Scrooby Separatists were calling themselves the Saints. They drew new members such as John Robinson. He was a minister who had left the Church of England rather than carry out King James's new rulings.

The meetings did not stay secret for long. With forty or fifty people meeting each Sunday at a landholding manor house, word was bound to leak out. By the fall of 1607, William Brewster was dismissed from his job as postmaster. Brewster and three others were called to appear before the Court of the High Commission in York, England. Though not jailed, they were fined for attending Separatist meetings.

Holland on the Horizon

The Gainsborough Separatists had already made plans to go to Amsterdam, Holland, and did so. There, they called themselves the Brethren of the Separation of the

First English Church at Amsterdam. Their minister was John Smyth, and they were generally called the Ancient Brethren. The Scrooby congregation made plans to also go to Holland. But how could they do so? According to a nine-year-old law prohibiting nonconformists to the Church of England from leaving the country, they would have to get a license from the king himself. Clearly, they had to leave England without this license. This would take planning. It would also take money that these simple farmers did not have.

THE FIRST EMIGRATION

"There was a large company of them proposed to get passage at Boston in Lincolnshire, and for that end had hired a ship wholly to themselves and made agreement with the master to be ready at a certain day . . ." writes William Bradford, in his book *Of Plymouth Plantation*, as he describes the Scrooby Separatists' first attempt to leave England.[1]

Arrested!

Plans had been made for Richard Clyfton and some of his congregation to travel on foot the sixty miles southeast to the seaport of Boston, England. The Separatists arrived on the appointed day and found no ship waiting for them. That night the ship arrived, and the captain took them on board. Then, according to William Bradford,

> he betrayed them, having before hand complotted [sic] with the searchers and other officers so to do; who took them [the Pilgrims], and put them into open boats, and there rifled and ransacked them, searching to their shirts for money, yea even the women further than became modesty . . .[2]

These officers of King James then took the Pilgrims back into Boston, made fun of them in front of the townspeople, and put them in prison. These simple farmers had no more money, and no way to legally defend against the thievery of the captain and their imprisonment. Within a month all were released except for seven men, including leader Richard Clyfton, John Robinson, and William Brewster.

Probably because these Separatist leaders were all rural ministers and nonministers, they were never brought to trial. They were released instead.

A New Plan

In the spring of 1608, this robbed and humiliated group of Separatists decided once again to leave for Holland. This time, the men would go ahead on foot for forty miles, and the women and children would follow by barge to the seacoast town of Hull. There were twenty to forty women and children.

Unfortunately, the barge of women and children arrived at Hull a full day before the ship that would take everyone to Holland. Seasick and tired, the women and children slept aboard the barge, which stayed in a nearby creek at low tide. By morning the barge was still aground—could not move from the mud—and the ship had arrived.

The Dutch captain of the ship, who did not want to be caught doing this illegal act, hustled the men on board. When he caught sight of an armed bunch of

---

SOURCE DOCUMENT

BUT THE POOR MEN WHICH WERE GOT ABOARD WERE IN
GREAT DISTRESS FOR THEIR WIVES AND CHILDREN. . . . IT
DREW TEARS FROM THEIR EYES, AND ANYTHING THEY HAD
THEY WOULD HAVE GIVEN TO HAVE BEEN ASHORE AGAIN. [3]

When the captain sailed his ship away, the women and children were left behind on the barge. William Bradford described how the Separatist men on the ship felt about being separated from their families.

men descending on the ship, the captain weighed anchor and sailed away.

The women who were left on the barge were arrested and taken, with their children, says Bradford "from one justice [judge] to another, till in the end they knew not what to do with them."[4] How could they imprison women and children who had committed no crime but to go with their husbands? They could not send them home, because all had sold their homes and everything in them to afford the trip. Bradford says that after all this trouble, the women and children were released and the authorities "were glad to be rid of them in the end upon any terms."[5]

The men who had been forced to sail away from their families encountered rough seas that drove them far north toward Norway. Even the sailors believed the ship would founder. The Pilgrims continued to pray, even when they thought the ship was sinking. The ship did not sink, and the storm stopped. They believed that their prayers had been answered and that God was with them. This faith was to get the Pilgrims through many a rough spot.

As Bradford says in his account of the trip to Holland, "And in the end, notwithstanding all these storms of opposition, they all got over at length, some at one time and some at another . . . and met together again . . . with no small rejoicing."[6]

Scrooby Farmers in Holland

In the early seventeenth century, Amsterdam was a town of two hundred forty thousand people. The Scrooby farmers spoke no Dutch and were not used to city life. However, their determination was still there. Here, in this foreign city, they could worship openly as they chose to do, not as the Church of England dictated they must.

With its large windmills and vast tulip fields, Holland was a strange place to the English Separatists. However, the country provided the Separatists with religious freedom.

The first problem was how to survive. The Saints began to learn trades. They became weavers, shoemakers, carpenters, barbers, printers, pipe makers, stone masons, tailors, hatters, glovers, button makers, and drapers. William Bradford made corduroy—a type of cloth.

All was not peaceful between the Ancient Brethren and the Scrooby Separatists. Since each church was able to interpret the Bible as it chose, this often led to quarrels about small differences in doctrine, or how one interprets a belief. There were even physical fights. This was hardly the peaceful, unified worship that the Separatists had wanted.

Uncomfortable in Amsterdam, about half of the members of the congregation decided, in 1609, to move to Leyden, a small cloth-manufacturing and university town. Any person had the right to live in Leyden, as long as he or she behaved well.

Richard Clyfton, the Separatists' minister, decided to stay in Amsterdam with the Ancient Brethren. John Robinson, who had gone to Leyden in 1609 to make way for the Separatists, joined his brother John Carver there. Robinson became the first Leyden minister.

Stink Alley

At Leyden, the small group of Saints still had trouble not starving. They worked for low wages and lived in a poor and crowded part of the city called *Stincksteeg*, which in English means "Stink Alley." The air was foul, and the sanitation was nonexistent. The infant death rate was high.

William Brewster had spent all of his money on helping the Separatists move to Holland. Brewster was no longer young, and working in a trade from sunrise to sunset would have been tough for him. Instead, he started giving private lessons in English to college students. He became sought after and successful, once again helping his fellow Saints as much as he could.

Despite all the problems, the Leyden congregation, which had started with twenty-one people, grew to over three hundred in about ten years. John Robinson ministered fairly and firmly.

The Separatist Church Service

The church services, which had been laughed at by the Church of England bishops for being joyless and severe, were just that. The men and women sat apart from each other on hard wooden benches. The children sat together, watched by deacons with long rods. If the children moved too much or talked, a deacon would use his rod to tap the offender firmly on the head.

The Separatists first stood and prayed for at least an hour. To pray on their knees was too much like the Church of England, and they would bow to no one but their God. John Robinson, their chosen pastor, then read a passage from the Bible, and the group sang—with no instruments accompanying them. The hymn was always sung by everyone together. (Part-singing was considered frivolous by these strict Christians.) Then there was a sermon that lasted for several hours. This was not delivered from a pulpit above the congregation, but from a wooden table on the same level as the benches. This emphasized the equality of the congregation with their chosen minister. One more song was sung, the collection plate was passed, and finally the benediction—or final spoken word—was given. This manner of holding a service continued on into Plymouth Colony.

After twelve years in Holland, some of the older members of the congregation worried that their children were becoming too Dutch. Also, the Dutch church, while certainly Protestant, was not as strict about Sunday worship as their own They resented its influence on their children. No matter how hard they worked, making more than a subsistence wage had proved impossible for most of these farmers-turned-craftsmen.

The Fugitive Brewster

In 1617, William Brewster started a printing business from a press in his home. Before long, Separatist pamphlets were being smuggled to England. The one that infuriated King James, whose bishops intercepted it, was called the "Perth Assembly." It was an attack on the Church of England written in 1578 by Laurence Chaderton. James gave orders that whoever printed this must be arrested and brought to him in England at once.

William Brewster, hearing that he was about to be arrested, went into hiding. He did not want to have his ear cut off and his nose split, and be whipped and sent to prison for life. This had already happened to

Alexander Leighten, who had also published some pamphlets critical of the Church.

The Separatists in Leyden were watched by English spies. They very much missed Brewster, the leading elder of their church. This, added to their other worries, caused them to think of leaving Leyden. Where could they go where they could be sure of having religious freedom, and where Brewster, now a fugitive, could join them?

The New World

Part of the congregation decided to try to travel to the New World, which included North and South America and the Caribbean. They discussed Virginia, having undoubtedly heard about the Jamestown Colony. Some people, perhaps having read Captain John Smith's 1616 book *A Description of New England*, began to consider that possibility. They had also heard of Guiana on the coast of South America, written about by Sir Walter Raleigh.

The Separatists knew that Jamestown was in great trouble and that many people had died there. They also knew that the investors of the London Company were actively looking for more settlers. King James was willing to send people unfriendly to his policies to Jamestown just to get rid of them. Perhaps he would feel the same about the Separatists.

Robert Cushman and John Carver, two deacons of the church, were sent to London to approach the London Company. Sir Edwin Sandys, who had known

*The Jamestown Colony was founded in Virginia in 1607.
John Smith, one of the colony's leaders, published the book* A
Description of New England *nine years later. The book got
many other Europeans interested in settling Virginia. For a
time, some of the Separatists wanted to settle in Virginia.*

William Brewster at Scrooby Manor, was a member of the London Company at that time. He was in favor of sending the Separatists to Virginia. They had knowledge of farming, which was sorely needed at Jamestown. However, King James, mad at the Separatists for defying him, would not agree to give them a grant of land or an official patent to settle in Virginia. He said they could go to Virginia and he would not bother them, but he refused to officially allow it. This upset the elders of the Leyden congregation. They did not trust King James and felt they had to look elsewhere for funding.

The Merchant Adventurers

In those days when mail traveled by ship, all of this back-and-forth wrangling took valuable time. In 1618, a member of the Ancient Brethren, Francis Blackwell, set out for Jamestown with two hundred followers. Their ship encountered terrible storms, got lost, and traveled around the South Atlantic Ocean for six months. By the time these Separatists arrived at Jamestown, one hundred fifty people had died, including Blackwell and all of the officers and sailors on the ship.

Disheartened but not discouraged by this appalling news, the hopeful Leyden Pilgrims continued to look for a patent and funding. Though they finally obtained a patent, the London Virginia Company was nearly bankrupt and could not fund them. The New Netherlands Company came into the picture, offering free transportation and livestock if the Separatists

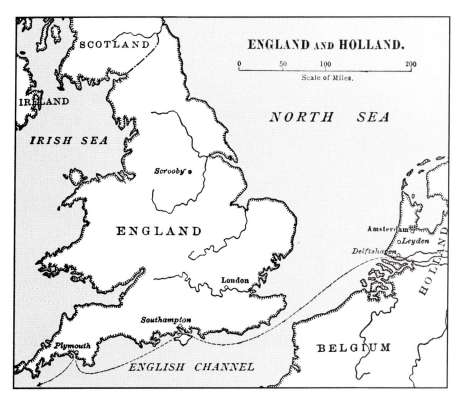

The English Separatists sought religious freedom first in nearby Holland. The arrow indicates the path the Pilgrims would later take on their way to the New World.

would settle at New Amsterdam (now New York City). Religious freedom went with this offer since it was a Dutch colony.

However, Thomas Weston told them he could borrow money and supplies from a group of London businessmen. There seemed to be no timetable for paying back this loan. Weston came up with a group of seventy men, mostly merchants from London, who formed a company called the Merchant Adventurers.

They would not interfere with the Pilgrims' religious beliefs or services. According to historians James Deetz and Patricia Scott Deetz, "The agreement stipulated that the adventurers would provide the capital for the planters in return for various commodities that would be sent from the colony back to England. In the case of Plymouth, these goods included furs, fish, clapboards, and sassafras."[7] The investors were encouraged to risk their money in the hope of making quick and large profits.

The Leyden congregation began to make plans. Who would be chosen to go on this journey? Who most wanted to go? Money for the journey and room on the ship were limited. Some would not go on the first trip, including Pastor Robinson. The youngest and strongest adults must have first choice. Many parents decided to leave their children in Leyden so they could prepare a home for them to join later.

After much debate about ten articles included in the contract, the Leyden Separatists decided to go with the Merchant Adventurers. Weston encouraged them to sail to Northern Virginia, which constituted the land between present-day Pennsylvania and Newfoundland, Canada. A patent for land in Northern Virginia was about to be issued to Sir Ferdinando Gorges, who headed a group of wealthy men calling themselves The Plymouth Company. This land in Northern Virginia would later be renamed New England. The problem was that the Pilgrims held a patent for Virginia itself, which was farther south than the land that Weston wanted them to settle.

Seventeenth Century New England

By the time the new plans were somewhat straightened out, the Separatists decided to land in New England. Some of the Merchant Adventurers had withdrawn because they preferred funding a trip to Virginia or Guiana. Quite a few of the Saints had also withdrawn.

England was very interested in tapping into the great fishing wealth that New England provided. Sir Ferdinando Gorges funded an exploratory trip by George Waymouth in 1605. Gorges and Waymouth wanted to start a fishing colony on the coast of present-day Maine. Though this did not take hold, Gorges sent Captain John Smith, who had helped establish the Jamestown Colony, to map the coast of New England. When Smith returned to England in 1614, he completed a map that would help the Pilgrims. He offered to accompany them on their trip. However, the Pilgrims preferred to follow his map without his presence. They told him that his book was a better bargain for their money than he was.

It seemed that the diminished bunch of Separatists was ready for an ocean voyage. Because of the fewer numbers, the Merchant Adventurers recruited more travelers in London. These new recruits were called the Strangers, and how the two groups would get along was still a mystery.

On July 21, 1620, a group of sad but determined Pilgrims set sail from Leyden to Delftshaven. Only three of these Pilgrims were from the original Scrooby congregation. William Brewster's wife, Mary, brought her two youngest sons with her. She hoped to be reunited with her fugitive husband. The arrangement

SETTING OUT FOR AMERICA

was that he would quietly board the ship, the *Speedwell*, in Southampton. The other two Scrooby Pilgrims were William Bradford and his wife, Dorothy, who left their five-year-old son with the Robinsons.

Early Troubles

The Pilgrims, who consisted of sixteen men, eleven women, and nineteen children, arrived at Delftshaven. There they saw two ships—the *Speedwell* and the *Mayflower*. The *Speedwell* looked awfully small to cross the huge Atlantic Ocean. It was only sixty tons; the *Mayflower* was three times that weight and about ninety feet long. The *Mayflower* was a "sweet ship." That is, it had been used to haul wine instead of fish.

Aboard the *Mayflower* were the Strangers, about forty-six people who were craftsmen and tradesmen and farmers wishing to forge a new life for themselves. Along with the Saints and the Strangers, there was a group of servants and hired men. Almost all of the Strangers and servants were members of the Church of England, with no desire to become

This replica of the Pilgrims' ship, the Mayflower, *is docked at Plymouth Harbor, Massachusetts.*

Separatists. Among the Strangers was John Alden, an exceptionally strong young man who came on board as a hired hand. Miles Standish, another Stranger, was a professional soldier.

The Saints and Strangers had to sort themselves and their possessions out on the docks of Southampton and then set sail, hopefully before the end of summer. Money was short and the Merchant Adventurers refused to advance more. The debt incurred with signing the contract meant that the Pilgrims would have to work very hard to pay off their high-interest loan from the company within the required seven years. All ready to set sail, there were still arguments over the provision in the contract that the houses and garden plots of the Pilgrims would be owned by the company. This meant that they would always be working for others. In the original contract, they were to have two days a week to work for their own families.

The contract was not at all pleasing to the Pilgrims. "The Leyden group bridled at this arrangement, and it had not been resolved in a satisfactory fashion at the time of their departure," according to historians James Deetz and Patricia Scott Deetz.[1]

Many of the Pilgrims did not want to sign the contract, but their agents did so quietly without letting the unsuspecting travelers know what they had agreed to. The result was that on August 5, 1620, the *Speedwell* and the *Mayflower* left Southampton harbor, carrying one hundred twenty passengers. All but about thirty people were on the *Mayflower*.

Almost immediately the tiny *Speedwell* began leaking. They docked in Dartmouth harbor for repairs, and set out again. This time around, the ship leaned over, nearly dumping its cargo, human and otherwise, into the harbor. By the time the ships had sailed into England's Plymouth harbor, it was apparent that the *Speedwell* was not going to the New World.

Everyone boarded the *Mayflower*, except for twenty people who could not, or just did not want to, crowd themselves and their possessions into such cramped quarters. Even Robert Cushman, the Pilgrims' first ambassador to the London Company, stayed behind.

The Problems With Each Other

The *Mayflower* set sail with 102 passengers on September 6, 1620. Immediately, an unforeseen problem arose. The thirty sailors on the ship disliked the Saints, and the feeling was returned. Nor did the Church of England Strangers like the Separatist Saints. The constant praying, led by William Brewster, who had been able to connect with the ship and leave his long exile, annoyed and frightened the Strangers. The Strangers felt these Separatists might be sinning against the king and against God. Elder Brewster was not even an ordained minister!

The Saints, on the other hand, believed that their constant praying was the only thing that kept the ship from sinking during several violent storms. They made it very clear that not only did they think their beliefs were right, but they intended to convince as many of the Strangers as they could to join their church.

On the Icy Cold Atlantic

The passengers on the *Mayflower* endured much discomfort during those sixty-six days. Though weather was good for several weeks, the first storm they encountered threw the seasick and frightened Pilgrims from side to side. The force of the storm was so severe that one of the main beams of the ship cracked. Someone had brought a large iron screw from Holland, and the crew members were able to mend the beam with it.

During another violent storm, John Howland was thrown overboard. Luckily, he was strong. He held on to ropes alongside the ship until he could be hauled aboard. According to William Bradford, "it pleased God that he caught hold of the topsail halyards which hung overboard and ran out at length."[2] Though ill from being in cold water for such a long time, Howland lived. Any time something fortunate happened, the Saints proclaimed it was because God was watching over them.

Passengers on deck were soaked with salt spray. Passengers below deck were treated to icy water as the seams of the ship leaked.

Life, however, went on. Elizabeth Hopkins, wife of Stephen Hopkins, gave birth to a boy they named Oceanus. Only one Pilgrim died before reaching land, a boy named William Butten, apprentice to surgeon Samuel Fuller.[3]

At last they reached land. It had taken them sixty-six days from Plymouth, ninety-eight days from Southampton, and for the Saints, four months from Delftshaven. Now they had reached the New World. Where were they?

Cape Cod is a narrow strip of land surrounding a harbor named for the abundance of codfish in its waters. The Cape also has many smaller harbors. On November 10, 1620, a day after spotting land, Captain Christopher Jones decided to sail along the ocean side of the Cape. Shoals, which are raging waters, soon enveloped the ship, and Captain Jones turned the ship to the northern end of Cape Cod.

THE MAYFLOWER COMPACT

The next morning the *Mayflower* was anchored in a good harbor (today the harbor of Provincetown). The ocean looked most uninviting that morning. The day was bleak and foggy. The sailors, never without an opinion where the Pilgrims were concerned, wanted them set ashore immediately. Then they demanded that Captain Jones set out for England in time to avoid winter weather.

The Strangers, tired of the Saints' praying and bossing them around, let it be known that they did not want to be in New England. The patents said they were to be in Virginia. When they got off the ship, they would go their own way.

Signing the Agreement

The Saints were smaller in number than the Strangers, the hired hands, the servants, and the sailors combined. Fortunately, among the Saints were strong leaders who were capable of writing up a document that aimed to assure all the tired, travel-weary Pilgrims that they would be treated fairly. After the first reading of the Mayflower Compact, which would be the governing principle of the colony, there was much discussion. When all felt, some grudgingly, that they could live

This mural on a monument in Provincetown, Massachusetts, depicts the signing of the Mayflower Compact.

with the words written, the signing began. John Carver signed first, then all the Saints. Only men could sign because women had no legal rights in 1620. Captain Miles Standish was the first Stranger to sign. The rest of the Strangers, first the ones with property, then the others, came next. Four out of the ten servants signed also.

With the signing of the Mayflower Compact, the tradition of direct election of leaders was born in America. John Carver was unanimously elected the first governor of Plymouth Colony.

Content of the Mayflower Compact

The compact was meant to stabilize these Pilgrims with their differing ideas about religion into a cooperative group. Since they had arrived at a place they had no legal right to be in and needed to find a place to form a colony before winter, this cooperation was necessary.

The Mayflower Compact starts out by stating that the people whose names are signed at the bottom are loyal subjects of King James. It continues on to say that these same subjects have voyaged to Northern Virginia for the glory of God, honor of king and country, and advancement of Christianity. These subjects plan to build the first colony in Northern Virginia (New England). In order to do this, "We . . . combine ourselves together into a civil body politic"[1]—in other words, they formed a group that will act together to form laws and constitutions and to elect officers.

SOURCE DOCUMENT

IN THE NAME OF GOD, AMEN.

WE, WHOSE NAMES ARE UNDERWRITTEN, THE LOYAL SUBJECTS OF OUR DREAD SOVEREIGN LORD KING JAMES, BY THE GRACE OF GOD OF GREAT BRITAIN, FRANCE, AND IRELAND, KING, DEFENDER OF THE FAITH, ETC, HAVING UNDERTAKEN FOR THE GLORY OF GOD AND ADVANCEMENT OF THE CHRISTIAN FAITH AND THE HONOR OF OUR KING AND COUNTRY, A VOYAGE TO PLANT THE FIRST COLONY IN THE NORTHERN PARTS OF VIRGINIA, DO BY THESE PRESENTS SOLEMNLY AND MUTUALLY, IN THE PRESENCE OF GOD, AND ONE ANOTHER, COVENANT AND COMBINE OURSELVES TOGETHER INTO A CIVIL BODY POLITIC, FOR OUR BETTER ORDERING AND PRESERVATION AND FURTHERANCE OF THE ENDS AFORESAID; AND BY VIRTUE HEREOF DO ENACT, CONSTITUTE, AND FRAME SUCH JUST AND EQUAL LAWS, ORDINANCES, ACTS, CONSTITUTIONS, AND OFFICERS FROM TIME TO TIME AS SHALL BE THOUGHT MOST MEET AND CONVENIENT FOR THE GENERAL GOOD OF THE COLONY ; UNTO WHICH WE PROMISE ALL DUE SUBMISSION AND OBEDIENCE. IN WITNESS WHEREOF WE HAVE HEREUNTO SUBSCRIBED OUR NAMES AT CAPE COD, THE 11TH OF NOVEMBER, IN THE YEAR OF THE REIGN OF OUR SOVEREIGN LORD KING JAMES OF ENGLAND, FRANCE, AND IRELAND, THE EIGHTEENTH, AND OF SCOTLAND THE FIFTY-FOURTH, ANNO DOMINI, 1620.

MR. JOHN CARVER	JOHN TURNER
WILLIAM BRADFORD	FRANCIS EATON
MR. EDWARD WINSLOW	JAMES CHILTON
MR. WILLIAM BREWSTER	JOHN CRACKSTON
MR. ISAAC ALLERTON	JOHN BILLINGTON
CAPT. MILES STANDISH	MOSES FLETCHER
JOHN ALDEN	JOHN GOODMAN
MR. SAMUEL FULLER	DEGORY PRIEST
MR. CHRISTOPHER MARTIN	THOMAS WILLIAMS
MR. WILLIAM MULLINS	GILBERT WINSLOW
MR. WILLIAM WHITE	EDMUND MARGESON
MR. RICHARD WARREN	PETER BROWN
JOHN HOWLAND	RICHARD BRITTERIDGE
MR. STEPHEN HOPKINS	GEORGE SOULE
EDWARD TILLY	RICHARD CLARKE
JOHN TILLY	RICHARD GARDINER
FRANCIS COOKE	JOHN ALLERTON
THOMAS ROGERS	THOMAS ENGLISH
THOMAS TINKER	EDWARD DOTEY
JOHN RIDGDALE	EDWARD LEISTER
EDWARD FULLER	

This is how the Mayflower Compact looks on a memorial tablet in Provincetown, Massachusetts. The original compact was handwritten.

The signers agreed to abide by the laws that they formed, so that the colony could be organized and self-preserving in order to achieve the lofty aims they have written of in the compact.

The Pilgrim leaders clearly saw the Mayflower Compact as necessary to the preservation of order as they tried to establish a colony in a strange land. According to historians James Deetz and Patricia Scott Deetz, however, the importance of this document has been exaggerated. It has become part of the myth of the Pilgrims, when it was actually a very practical move, and not a "forerunner to the U.S. Constitution."[2] "This is not," write the Deetzes, "to decry the fact that the basis of Plymouth government was a belief in the rule of law, not nearly as clearly formulated as it is today, but visibly present in what can be seen by 1671 as an embryonic [early form of the] bill of rights."[3]

Exploring the New Land

November 11, 1620, when the compact was signed, was the very first day the Pilgrims set foot on the soil of New England. Sixteen men, armed against possible attack by the American Indians, went ashore to get firewood and water. November 12 was spent on the boat since it was the Sabbath, a holy day. On the morning of November 13, the entire company came onshore, under an armed guard. The women did the washing, and children raced around on the beach. Men worked on the long boat and the shallop. Clams and mussels were found on the beach. Unfortunately the mussels made those who ate them very ill.

There was no fresh water for settling at this spot. Winter was coming soon and the weather was becoming chilly. Again, sixteen men armed themselves and went deep into the woods to explore. Among these men were William Bradford and Miles Standish. As strong and brave as these men were, they had never trekked through a wilderness before. They saw some American Indians who immediately turned and went

Sixteen Pilgrims began preparing their settlement by gathering firewood in the cold New England air. To them, the possibility of American Indian attack was always a concern.

farther into the woods. The Pilgrims tried to follow them but did not find them.

The exploratory party spent a very cold night out in the open. In the morning, they continued to search for the American Indians in the hills and deep ravines of the countryside. The explorers were tired, cold, and thirsty. They finally found a spring of fresh water, and shortly after that discovered cornfields and an American Indian grave. They also found mounds of earth that were used by the American Indians for burying corn for seed. The corn was in several baskets. Coming across a kettle, they poured the corn into the kettle and proceeded to haul it away with them. The Pilgrims did not see this as a theft, but rather felt that God had provided the corn.

Back to Corn Hill

During the ten days that the company lived on the boat and came on shore by day, the necessary repairs were made and the weather became colder. The Pilgrims needed a permanent settlement. Led by Captain Jones, twenty-four Pilgrims and nine sailors set out in the shallop to explore what is now called the Truro region of Cape Cod. The shallop being forced to turn back by bad weather, some of the men were stranded on shore. They had to await the shallop's return the next day. Though chilled and weakened, those on shore rejoined the exploring party the next day. The group returned to what they now called Corn Hill.

SOURCE DOCUMENT

THERE WAS A VARIETY OF OPINIONS AMONGST US ABOUT THE EMBALMED PERSON. SOME THOUGHT IT WAS AN INDIAN LORD AND KING; OTHERS SAID THE INDIANS ALL HAVE BLACK HAIR AND NEVER ANY WAS SEEN WITH BROWN OR YELLOW HAIR. SOME THOUGHT IT WAS A CHRISTIAN OF SPECIAL NOTE WHO HAD DIED AMONGST THEM, AND THEY BURIED HIM THUS TO HONOR HIM. OTHERS THOUGHT THEY HAD KILLED HIM AND HAD DONE IT IN TRIUMPH OVER HIM . . ."[4]

The writer of Mourt's Relation *explains how the Pilgrims had talked about the strange body on Corn Hill.*

There, they found more corn and an interesting grave that contained the remains of a child and a man with yellow hair. The man was wrapped in a sailor's canvas and had on cloth breeches (trousers).

(According to historian H. Roger King, the yellow hair of the body, clearly a chief or man of importance among the Indians, was "the result of the chemical reaction of the red ochre embalming powder on the Indian's white hair, and the European clothing came from some French sailors shipwrecked on the Cape a few years earlier."[5] In other words, King felt that this was an American Indian grave.)

The Pilgrims took the artifacts in the grave, knives and needles, and helped themselves to dried beans and more corn. The food would be needed during the rapidly approaching winter months.

First Encounter

Still another exploring party set out in the shallop, including Bradford, Standish, Edward Winslow, and Governor Carver. They saw American Indians working on something black on the shore. Upon seeing the white men in the shallop, the Indians ran away, shouting and gesturing. The company stayed on the beach that night, having built a fire. In the morning, they discovered that the black object was a grampus, a kind of small whale. The exploring party then tracked the American Indians, passing formal burial grounds. Again they camped, and "About midnight we heard a great and hideous cry, and our sentinel called *Arm, Arm,*" according to *Mourt's Relation*.[6] However, the noise stopped shortly after it began.

While they were having breakfast very early on the morning of December 8, they heard more of the same sounds. "One of our company . . . came running in and cried, *They are men! Indians! Indians!*"[7] The Pilgrims picked up their firearms and barricaded themselves behind the shallop. Miles Standish was the first to shoot. The American Indians howled and shot arrows. The Pilgrims fired back with their muskets. Neither Pilgrims nor Indians were hurt, and the Indians finally fled into the woods.

The Pilgrims named the place where this encounter occurred "the First Encounter." This spot is still marked on present-day road maps of Cape Cod.

The Myth of Plymouth Rock

The exploring party sailed on all that day, to Plymouth, named by Captain John Smith in 1614. They stopped on Clark's Island in Plymouth Harbor and then went ashore on the mainland. Legend tells us that this was when the Pilgrims landed at Plymouth Rock. It was more likely Plymouth Harbor, according to historians James Deetz and Patricia Scott Deetz.[8]

The date of the landing was December 11, according to our modern calendar, which is ten days further

Having landed at Plymouth to start a new colony, the Pilgrims faced an uncertain future in the New World.

This depiction of the Pilgrims landing at Plymouth shows the colonists meeting an American Indian right away. In reality, the Pilgrims would not be greeted by friendly Indians until after starting their settlement.

into the year than the old calendar in use until 1752. Eighteen men of the exploring party liked Plymouth and its harbor, and they decided that this would be the best place to settle.

A Fine Place for a Colony

Arriving back at the ship with the news, William Bradford was greeted with a tragedy. Somehow, his wife, Dorothy, had fallen from the anchored ship and drowned. Bradford, in his journal, notes only, under the heading "Deaths:" "Dec. 7. Dorothy, Wife to Mr. William Bradford."[9] The cold, the hunger, the newness and strangeness of this land had made many of the Pilgrims sad and disappointed. It is possible that Dorothy Bradford ended her own life.[10] Since this was considered a sin by Saints and Strangers alike, no mention of it would have been made.

Once again, the Pilgrims debated where they would land. They finally agreed to trust the exploring party and set sail for Plymouth. They arrived at Plymouth Harbor on December 16. They observed the already farmed areas, proving that Plymouth had once been an American Indian village. There was a freshwater brook and a high hill facing the shore where they could build a fort.

This small band of people was now starting a colony. The Mayflower Compact would help them deal with each other. By December 20, the Pilgrims had decided where their town was to be built. They began to build houses on Christmas Day 1620.

Since the Saints did not celebrate Christmas or other Christian holidays, they simply ignored any grumbling from the Strangers as they set to work on the very first Pilgrim building, the Common House. It was most important to have shelter before winter became colder and snowier. Already billowing snow and sleet made it difficult to build. People still slept aboard the *Mayflower*, and it took time to go back and forth from ship to shore. As more and more people became ill, the Common House became a hospital for men too sick to go back to the ship after their day's work.

THE HOWLING OF WOLVES

New Plimoth

New Plimoth, as the town was named, was first a short street that rose steeply from the beach and was laid out along the brook for several hundred yards. It ended at Fort Hill, where Miles Standish placed the largest cannon. Lots allowing eight and one quarter square feet for each family member, thus having a minimum of sixteen and a half square feet for a

The winter having already begun, the Pilgrims tried to build houses for themselves as quickly as possible.

married couple, were marked along the street. Nineteen buildings housed married couples, their children, and one or more single men. Who got which piece of property was randomly determined, and all agreed upon this planned community.

The south side of the street was used for houses. The other side was reserved for the cornfields, with the exception of the houses of the governor and Stephen Hopkins that were built the first winter. When the land was later turned into lots, Standish was given the house closest to Fort Hill so that he could get to the cannon quickly. But during the first weeks and months, it was important to get housed as fast as possible. Smoke from American Indian fires could be seen in the distance and a few Indian huts had been discovered in the woods.

Getting Lost in the American Wilderness

In early January 1621, Peter Browne and John Goodman, who had gone to the woods to gather thatch for roofing, disappeared. A search party thrashed around the woods until night fell. Browne and Goodman did not return that night or the following day. When they did return, they told a chilling tale of getting lost while hunting deer, and then having to spend the night in freezing rain. As they started to fall asleep, they heard what they thought were "two lions roaring exceedingly for a long time together."[1] Of course, this ended their sleep for the night. The rest of the night, they paced about under a tree, which they could climb for safety if necessary. By the time they came home, their shoes had to be cut from their feet, which were swollen from the damp and cold.

Goodman, who seemed to wander off a great deal, limped into the woods with his gun a short time later and surprised a couple of wolves that tried to attack his dog. The dog escaped, as did Goodman, who now recognized the sound of howling wolves, which he had mistaken for lions.

"The General Sickness"

Though American Indian alarms and howling creatures could be handled, the lack of adequate shelter added to the illness that was invading the colony. Those who had survived the ocean crossing began to see their loved ones sicken and die. The Pilgrims called it "The General Sickness"—and it was probably pneumonia or tuberculosis, both diseases of the lungs. This was made worse by scurvy, caused by not eating fresh fruits or vegetables on the long voyage.

By the end of March, almost half of the original Pilgrims were dead. People were burying their dead at night so the American Indians would not know how weak the colony had become. Only five of the eighteen married women were still alive, and only ten of the twenty-nine unmarried men. Also, half of the sailors had died. Miles Standish's wife and Edward Winslow's wife died. William White, father of the first baby born in New England, Peregrine White, died, though his wife and children survived. Only three families, William Brewster's among them, were left intact by the end of winter.

An American Indian Scare

American Indians were spotted in the woods on February 16, 1621. A hunter, unidentified in William Bradford's journal, saw twelve American Indians marching toward the settlement.[2] He hid himself, hearing more American Indians in the woods, then sped home to raise the alarm. No American Indians appeared at Plymouth, though a large fire could be seen through the woods. Captain Standish and Francis Cooke had left their tools in the woods when the

American Indian alarm came. When they went back to the spot where they had been working, they discovered the tools had been taken.

This alarm caused the colony to call a meeting where they elected Miles Standish the commander in chief of the Pilgrim forces. During their meeting, two American Indians appeared on a hill, beckoning the men to come to them. The Pilgrims beckoned in their turn, hearing many more Indians over the hill. Neither Pilgrims nor Indians would make the move to go forward, so no parley, or negotiations, took place.

Captain Jones brought a great cannon onshore on February 21, and it and other guns were set on bases on Fort Hill. All this time the Pilgrims, who were not hunters or fishermen, were trying their best to shoot game and get ready to fish when the winter was over. Though starvation was not what killed so many of the Pilgrims, constant hunger and poor nutrition weakened everyone. Seeds could not be planted until the ground had thawed.

The Great Samoset

On March 16, 1621, the Pilgrims were engaged in a business meeting in the Common House. A lone brave, or American Indian man, presented himself at the door, about to march right in. Even more amazing, this bold brave spoke to the shocked Pilgrims in English!

After gathering their wits, the astonished Pilgrims questioned the brave, called Samoset. They found out

Miles Standish commanded the Pilgrims' tiny army. He had already had military experience in England.

that he was an *Abnaki sagamore*—or "lord"—from Monhegan Island, about ten miles out into the Atlantic from the coastline of present-day Maine.

Samoset had sailed with English captains along the Newfoundland coast (north of Maine in present-day Canada) and had learned English. From Samoset, the Pilgrims learned that Plymouth was originally called Patuxet by the American Indians. It had been an American Indian village where a great plague had killed all who lived there. He also told them about a Wampanoag Indian chief named Massasoit. The Wampanoag village was on Narragansett Bay, forty miles southwest of Plymouth.

Samoset was happy to talk with the Pilgrims and be fed. He was totally naked except for a cloth between his legs. The Pilgrims quickly offered him a long red coat—to keep him warm they said, but possibly because they were embarrassed by his nudity. "We would gladly have been rid of him at night, but he was not willing to go this night," wrote the author of *Mourt's Relation*.[3] They lodged him at Stephen Hopkins's house "and watched him."[4] The first face-to-face encounter with the supposedly dangerous American Indians had been nothing like the Pilgrims expected.

Samoset departed the following morning with gifts of a knife, a bracelet, and a ring. The next day, he came back with five braves carrying beaver skins. This was good news to the Pilgrims, for beaver fur was valuable and could help them pay off their debt to the Merchant

Adventurers. These American Indians also brought back the tools stolen from the woods. Samoset stayed, and the Pilgrims sent the five braves back to their village with presents for more skins.

Squanto

This time, the braves did not return as quickly. When four days had passed, the Pilgrims sent Samoset to find them. He had told the Pilgrims about a tribe called the Nausets, living southeast of Plymouth. These American Indians, with about one hundred braves in the village, were very angry at the English because of a ship's captain named Thomas Hunt. He had captured twenty Patuxet men and seven Nausets. Captain Hunt then sold these American Indians in England as slaves.

Before Samoset returned, several American Indians appeared on the hills around Plymouth and made threatening gestures. Captain Standish prepared for a battle that never came. On March 22, Samoset reappeared with four braves, one of whom was called Squanto. Squanto was one of the twenty captives who had been taken off into slavery by Captain Hunt.

Before he was captured by Hunt, however, Squanto was captured by Captain Waymouth. According to most sources, Squanto came back to New England with Captain John Smith in 1614, only to be captured again by Hunt. This time, Spanish friars bought him. The resourceful Squanto, now speaking English and Spanish, managed to escape to

England where he lived with John Slanie. Slanie was treasurer of the Newfoundland Company, which had fishing interests in New England.

It is most likely that Squanto again returned in one of the Newfoundland Company's ships. He then met a Captain Dermer who was in the employ of Sir Ferdinando Gorges, in 1618. It was on Dermer's ship that Squanto returned home to Massachusetts—only to find that all of his family, in fact his entire village of Patuxet, had died in the great plague. He then presented himself to Massasoit at Sowams and was allowed to make his home with the Wampanoag.

William Bradford has said that Squanto was "a speciall [sic] instrumente [sic] sent of God for their good beyond their expectation."[5] Squanto had found the home he really wanted, and he became a true Saint in the eyes of the Separatists, eventually adopting their religion.

Massasoit and the Wampanoag

The very first day Squanto was introduced to the Pilgrims, word came that Massasoit was beyond the hills with sixty Wampanoag braves. They were a delegation, however, and not a war party. Captain Standish still assembled his little army complete with armor and steel weapons.

Then, they sent Squanto out to talk with this delegation. Squanto came back, saying that one of the Pilgrim leaders should go out to parley with the Indians. Edward Winslow was sent to sound out the

Wampanoag and to assure them that peace and trade was all the Pilgrims wanted. Gifts such as knives and a copper chain with a jewel, "strong water" (some kind of alcoholic beverage), biscuits, and butter were sent along with Winslow.

The gifts were accepted. Winslow then made a speech about the love and peace sent by King James, and how much the colony wanted to be friends and trade with the American Indians. Massasoit liked the speech, and very much admired the armor worn by Winslow. He wished to buy it and Winslow's sword. Winslow gently declined.

Massasoit left Winslow with his brother, Quadequina, and crossed the brook "with some twenty men who left all their bows and arrows behind. We kept six or seven of them as hostages for our messenger," according to *Mourt's Relation*.[6]

Standish met Massasoit at the brook, and gradually the Wampanoag came to a building where the Pilgrims sat them on their best cushions. Governor Carver then arrived in grand style, with drum and trumpet heralding his entrance. Much saluting and kissing of hands (as a way of greeting) took place. The Pilgrims and Wampanoag ate and drank, then the negotiations began.

A Treaty With the Wampanoag

A treaty emerged from all of this ritualized friendliness. The Wampanoag were often at war with the Narragansett Indian federation. An alliance with the English would be helpful to the Wampanoag if they were

Massasoit brought an impressive delegation of braves with him when he came to meet the Pilgrims for the first time.

attacked by the Narragansett. The Pilgrims did not know about this extra reason for the Wampanoag to seek an alliance, and the Wampanoag did not know how close to disaster this little colony really was.

The Pilgrims agreed to pay the Wampanoag, in trade goods, for the corn they had stolen. The Wampanoag agreed to return some metal farming tools stolen a few weeks previous to this meeting. Both sides agreed to punish their own people if they offended the other side. Most importantly, each group agreed to help defend the other from outside attack. This treaty was to last for fifty years.

Squanto Is a Great Help

On March 23, 1621, the Wampanoag delegation left for their village at Sowams. Edward Winslow was returned to Plymouth, and the Wampanoag hostages rejoined their tribe. Though various members of the tribe stayed around for several days, hoping for more food and drink, no incidents occurred. The Pilgrims began to believe that Massasoit really did want to have peace with this small colony. Squanto and Samoset stayed at Plymouth. Since the Pilgrims had not been successful at catching fish and other seafood, Squanto decided to teach them. He began by bringing them many eels, which he caught with his feet.

Winter was at an end, and most of the sickness had passed. Corn could now be planted. John Carver was reelected to serve as governor for the coming year. (According to the old-style calendar, the Pilgrims' New Year's Day was on March 25.) It was also nearing the time when the *Mayflower* would return to England, minus half its sailors and with little in the hold to help pay off the Pilgrims' debts to the Merchant Adventurers.

The *Mayflower* sailed on April 5, and barely a week later, John Carver died. William Bradford was elected governor, with Isaac Allerton his assistant.

Squanto taught the Pilgrims how to plant and fertilize corn and how to catch herring, as well as eels. Squanto also taught them how to tap the abundant maple trees for sap. He helped them find and trap deer and other game. The Pilgrims spent the spring busily planting.

Life Goes On

The very first wedding in Plymouth occurred on May 12, 1621, when Edward Winslow, whose wife had died that winter, married Susanna White, whose husband had also died. This was a civil wedding ceremony because the Pilgrims did not believe that weddings were religious events.

The first summer in New England saw the Pilgrims' corn growing with abundance, though their English grains did not do well. Berries and grapes gave them nutrients that they had not known before. The Pilgrims were always working, eating on the run, and there was still barely enough food to keep them alive until harvest. They learned to find and pick wild leeks, watercress, and nuts, and to dry fruit and make wine. People in the seventeenth century did not drink as much water as modern-day Americans do. Even babies, after they were weaned, drank beer. But when the beer ran out, and before they were able to make wine, these Pilgrims had to make do with the water from the brook.

The Hungry Braves

During the spring and summer of 1621, the daily life of the Pilgrims was often interrupted by American Indians wandering around the village, entering their homes, and cheerfully asking to be fed. This finally became so dangerous to their slim food supplies, that Edward Winslow and Stephen Hopkins were sent, with Squanto as interpreter, to Massasoit's village. They were to ask the chief to convince his people to visit less.

All along the way to Sowams, Winslow and Hopkins met American Indians who shared their food with them. By the time they arrived at Sowams, there was not much food in the village. Massasoit said he understood the difficulty he caused by bringing so many people to visit. He also agreed to give the Pilgrims seed corn and to trade with them for furs.

Winslow and Hopkins were invited to spend the night, not realizing that this meant they would share a few wooden planks with the chief, his wife, several braves, and assorted lice and fleas. To add to this, the Wampanoag had a habit of singing themselves to sleep, and every so often yet another brave would come and add himself to the pile.[7]

This went on for two nights, and two very tired and hungry Pilgrims left for Plymouth as soon as possible. The American Indians, who were generous with food when they had it, were used to going for a long time without it. This was just one of the many misunderstandings that occurred due to the different cultures of the Englishmen and the American Indians.

The First Thanksgiving

By summer, the hungry feeling that had always been with the Pilgrims began to fade. The corn ripened and they had learned more about native plants and how to hunt and fish well.

The Wampanoag typically lived in this type of lodge.

The time came when they sent the shallop to trade for beaver pelts with the Wampanoag. The Pilgrims hoped they could send back to England a large quantity of valuable goods the next time a boat arrived.

During the autumn of 1621, the Pilgrims' harvest of corn was beyond all expectations. They decided to set aside a day of thanksgiving for a harvest festival, the closest thing to a party the Saints would ever allow. This first Thanksgiving Day was in October 1621.

Squanto was sent to invite Massasoit and his braves to the feast. Every Pilgrim household prepared dishes from their gardens, and four men went out to shoot

Both Pilgrims and American Indians provided and shared the vast amounts of food on the first Thanksgiving.

ducks, geese, and wild turkeys. There were so many of these that the Pilgrims, who numbered only about sixty people after the hard winter, were sure they would eat well for a week.

Then Massasoit arrived. With him were ninety hungry braves. How could the Pilgrims feed all of these men and have enough for themselves to eat? Massasoit once again understood the situation and sent some of his braves into the forest to kill deer. The men returned with five deer to add to the feast, which continued for three days! This was truly a joining of the two cultures in this abundant land.

7

BETRAYAL AND THE THREAT OF WAR

So much had happened in less than a year. Many had died, but hope was strong. The harvest had been promising and the chances of the Pilgrims going into the next winter strong and healthy looked good. Still, this little colony was quite alone on a shore surrounded by wilderness, and they were on friendly terms with only one tribe of American Indians. With so few people, could they withstand an attack if it happened?

New Settlers

On November 11, 1621, reinforcements to the small colony arrived. A ship was sighted in Plymouth Harbor. It was the *Fortune*, which had sailed from London in July, and it brought thirty-five new Pilgrims who wanted to settle at Plymouth. Family members who had been left behind during the first crossing came off the ship: William Brewster's son Johnathan, now twenty-eight, and Edward Winslow's younger brother. Also on board was Robert

Cushman, one of the Saints' beloved deacons, with his fourteen-year-old son, Thomas.

Important letters also arrived with the *Fortune*. Some of these brought better news than others. The good news was that Sir Ferdinando Gorges had signed a patent reorganizing the Plymouth Company, which promised the Pilgrims that at the end of seven years, each would receive a grant of one hundred acres of land.

The bad news was that Thomas Weston insisted that the Pilgrims actually sign the contract that somehow had not been signed in the rush to sail. (Who actually agreed to the contract with the Merchant Adventurers and whether it was in writing before the Pilgrims left England is something historians do not know for sure.) But now, warned Weston, if a written contract was not signed, the Pilgrims could forget about getting any more money or supplies.

Deacon Cushman delivered a sermon urging the Pilgrims to sign the contract. This meant that the Pilgrims, whose first year had been spent barely surviving, would have to send a great many valuable goods such as lumber, fish, and furs back to England to pay off their debt. In return, the Merchant Adventurers would continue to send supplies that the Pilgrims could not generate for themselves.

Robert Cushman left with the *Fortune* in December 1621, the hold filled with lumber and beaver pelts. These were worth about five hundred pounds, about half of what the Pilgrims still owed their sponsors. William Bradford and Edward Winslow also sent back a manuscript that told about the Pilgrims' first year on Cape Cod.

The *Fortune's* Bad Luck

Unfortunately, the *Fortune* was captured by French pirates just as it reached the English Channel. All of the valuable goods that the Pilgrims had spent so much time and effort to gather were stolen. Luckily for those aboard, the ship was finally allowed to sail to London. Cushman informed Weston of the loss, and delivered the manuscript to a printer. It was not considered valuable enough to steal!

This manuscript, published under the name of G. Mourt, came to be known as *Mourt's Relation*. It was distributed and read in England. This book, which stressed adventure over hardship, helped interest other people in coming to colonize New England.

The Pilgrims and the American Indians

However, the Pilgrims could not know of the fate of the *Fortune* as it sailed away in December 1621. They had other things to worry about. Their generally good relationship with the American Indians was about to be disrupted. The Narragansett Indian tribe was very powerful, controlling almost all of what is now Rhode Island. The tribe was reported to have thirty thousand members, five thousand of whom were fighting braves. At Plymouth there were still only about fifty men who could bear arms. The Narragansett were enemies of the Massachuset and constantly threatened the Wampanoag. Canonicus, chief of the Narragansett, challenged Plymouth to a battle. A Narragansett runner brought a sheaf of arrows wrapped in a snake skin for Squanto, who was not in the village. The runner left these for Governor Bradford, who captured the runner and ordered him held until Squanto returned and could interpret.

The runner was terrified. However, when he realized his life was not at stake, he began to tell his story. Hopkins and Winslow listened intently. Both of them had learned some American Indian words and were used to negotiating with the Indians. Evidently, a representative of the Narragansett had come to Plymouth to talk about peace terms. And that messenger had returned to Canonicus saying that the Pilgrims preferred war! Perhaps the Narragansett ambassador had not received a present he liked—but *this* messenger would be sure to go back to Canonicus and talk about peace. Bradford and Standish decided that this man had no authority to keep a promise, and might be lying anyway. He was not the person to negotiate with.

The snake skin was filled with powder and shot and sent back to the chief of the Narragansett. Canonicus was so appalled by the sight of this open threat that he refused even to touch it. The messenger would not have any more to do with it, either.

The snake skin traveled around the village for a few weeks. It finally came back to Plymouth, never having been opened![1]

The Threat of War

No peace had been called for, and rumors of imminent attack on Plymouth continued. Governor Bradford decided that the colony must become a fortress. For six weeks, barricades of heavy timber were cut, shaped, and used to build a palisade (a fence of stakes) around the town and Fort Hill. Four strong supports called bastions were built at the corners of the fortified walls. Here lookouts could see for miles, and gates were built into three of the bastions. These gates were kept locked and guarded.

Standish formed his fifty Pilgrims into four companies. Each company had a leader who planned the defenses of a particular part of the settlement. One whole company was responsible for dealing with the fire-arrows that the Narragansett might send into the wooden fort.

A friendly American Indian named Hobomok, who had helped Captain Standish in an earlier nonthreatening incident, reported that the Massachuset Indians of Boston Bay had decided to join the Narragansett. The Massachuset Indians would surround Standish and his men the next time they came out of the fort. Then, the Narragansett would attack the weakened settlement. Hobomok also said that Squanto had agreed to help in this conspiracy!

Besides being able to keep an eye out for American Indians in the thick New England woods, guards at Fort Hill also had a good view of Plymouth Harbor.

The Pilgrims did not believe this last rumor. Squanto had helped the Pilgrims survive in their wilderness home. How could this be true?

There was much discussion among the Pilgrim leaders. It was decided that there was no point barricading themselves in the fort, for they were running out of food and needed to trade with friendly American Indians. They would test out the accuracy of the rumor about the Massachuset Indians by going to trade with them, as had been already arranged.

Miles Standish—with ten settlers, Squanto, and Hobomok—set out in the shallop. Before they had sailed far, an American Indian who knew Squanto came running down to the beach, bleeding from his face. He urged the men to return to Plymouth, saying that Massasoit's men had joined the Narragansett and they were going to attack the settlement. Standish returned at once to Plymouth, which was readying itself for attack.

Squanto's Betrayal

Hobomok was very offended that Standish could think Massasoit would join the Wampanoag's enemies to attack the Pilgrims. It was all caused by Squanto, he was sure, who wanted to get the tribes angry at each other. Hobomok offered to send his wife to visit Massasoit's wife and see what was going on in Sowams.

Hobomok's wife found everything peaceful in Sowams. She told Massasoit why she was there and described the panic that the rumors had caused at Plymouth. Massasoit immediately sent her back to Plymouth to tell Bradford that the Wampanoag were still totally at peace with the Pilgrims. He also could not imagine anything could have happened to Squanto's friend or relative who was bleeding on the beach. Furthermore, if he heard of any such attacks he would immediately send a warning to Plymouth.

As unbelievable as it seemed, Squanto was the culprit. In order to receive excellent presents from various American Indian villages, he had told them that the settlers planned to kill them—and only he, Squanto, had enough influence to talk the Pilgrims into peace. This had been going on for some time, and Squanto had become quite powerful as a perceived protector of the American Indian tribes.[2]

Bradford sent messages to all tribes concerned. He said that the Pilgrims' intentions were only peaceful and that the tribes should never believe anything else that Squanto had to say about it. The local chiefs, including Massasoit himself, demanded that the Pilgrims put Squanto to death—or turn him out of the village so they could see to it themselves!

Bradford was grateful to Squanto for past help and also knew that he could be of great use in the future. He simply told Squanto what he thought of his behavior and that he would be dealt with much more harshly if he ever tried anything like that again.

A Wish for Squanto's Death

Trading went on as before, but the American Indians were not so forgiving as the governor had been. Massasoit himself came to Plymouth to demand that Squanto be put to death. Massasoit left Plymouth angry that Bradford had not agreed with him. He sent a messenger back to Plymouth reminding Bradford of the terms of peace the Wampanoag and the English had signed in March 1621: "And if any of

Massasoit demanded that the Pilgrims uphold their treaty with the Wampanoag and have Squanto put to death for his betrayal. Here, Massasoit holds a peace pipe, which may have been smoked after the Pilgrims and Wampanoag agreed to their treaty.

his did hurt to any of theirs, he should send the offender, that they might punish him."[3] Massasoit even sent along a knife with which Governor Bradford could kill Squanto, personally. Bradford then only had to send Squanto's severed head and hands to Massasoit.

What could Bradford do? The peace terms with the Wampanoag were very valuable to the Pilgrims. Reluctantly, he agreed to send Squanto to Massasoit's village at Sowams. A boatload of American Indians

The Pilgrims, as well as other early American settlers, built wattle-and-daub houses. These types of houses were built by laying a mat of woven rods and sticks over a wooden frame, then plastering the mat with clay.

arrived to take him away. The braves refused to come to get Squanto, demanding that the Pilgrims bring him across the bay to their boat. Bradford was suspicious that these might not be Wampanoag Indians at all, but enemy braves. When he demanded evidence that they had been sent by Massasoit, the braves rowed away angrily.

It seems that one of Squanto's stories that he spread among the American Indians was that the English had barrels of plague under their storehouse. One of the Pilgrims had told Hobomok that even if there was no plague kept under the storehouse, the American Indians were not safe. The Pilgrim said that the English God was so strong that he kept some plague stored up in heaven that he could, and would, send down to fell his enemies.[4] Having already seen how smallpox could kill their people, the American Indians believed this story. This ended the desire to take Squanto away, and despite further evidence of his double-dealing, he was not sent from Plymouth either. He would prove still valuable as a guide and as an interpreter with tribes who did not know of his treachery.

Thomas Weston Causes Trouble

With the immediate threat of American Indian warfare over and Squanto under control, the Pilgrims could turn their attention to trading. It was very important to them that they pay the debt owed to the Merchant Adventurers as quickly as possible. In

March 1622, Standish and Squanto took a small company in the shallop to the Massachuset Indians. This trading went well, but once again the colony was short of food.

The new settlers who arrived on the *Fortune* had done more to diminish supplies than add to them. Thomas Weston, despite the Pilgrims having signed the contract, sent no ships with food for the winter. Weston and the Merchant Adventurers had not received the Pilgrims' payment because it had been stolen from the *Fortune*. Not knowing of the *Fortune's* capture, the Pilgrims must have wondered why no food and supplies had arrived by ship. By April, before crops could be harvested, food was very scarce. They had exhausted their supply of trade goods and faced starvation once again.

To make matters worse, at the end of May, a shallop appeared in the harbor carrying seven Englishmen and letters from Thomas Weston. There was no food on board, and the seven men expected the Pilgrims to feed them. It seems Weston was no longer one of the Merchant Adventurers, and no more help would come from him. In addition, he was starting a settlement and trading post of his own at Wessagusset (now Weymouth), on Boston Bay.

Weston also told them that the rest of the Pilgrims at Leyden were not going to be transported to Plymouth because they were too poor to contribute to shares in the company. There was also a letter from a Captain Huddleston, who told of a massacre led by Opechancanough, the chief sachem of the Paspahegh Indians in Jamestown, Virginia. There, on March 22, three hundred fifty settlers had been massacred. After hearing news of the massacre, the Pilgrims hurried to shore up the fort that they had started building.

Still more was to come. Two ships filled with sixty of Weston's men showed up on June 22, 1622. They brought no food and expected the Pilgrims to feed them until they could go on to Weston's colony. These men proved to be coarse and rude and no help at all to the settlement. The generous Pilgrims actually shared their food with these intruders. However, all supplies were kept under guard and anyone caught stealing corn from the fields was whipped.

Weston's men left Plymouth in the fall of 1622, hearing that a site had been found at Wessagusset. News from Boston Bay came back to the Pilgrims from American Indians. It was not good. Weston's rude men were making enemies of the American Indians, treating them savagely.

Starvation Looms

Despite the terrible summer, Plymouth hosted its second wedding—that of John Alden, tall and strong and twenty-three years old, to twenty-year-old Priscilla Mullens, whose parents had died in the first winter's sickness. This was a marriage successful not only in life, but also in literature.[5] A poem, "The Courtship of Miles Standish," by Henry Wadsworth Longfellow was written in 1858 and mythologizes Mullens, Alden, and Standish.

The fall harvest of 1622 was not a good one. Despite the Pilgrims' disapproval of the methods used by the Wessagusset settlers, they agreed to join Weston's company in a trading effort to the American Indians, this time to obtain food. It was on this expedition, in December 1622, that Squanto died. Left without an interpreter in the middle of the trip, Bradford returned to Plymouth and traded with local American Indians as well as he could.

The threat of famine became very real in the winter of 1623. This was true not only for the Plymouth Colony, but also for the new settlement at Wessagusset. The Massachuset Indians, tired of their treatment by Weston's men, had refused to supply the new settlement with any more corn. Governor John Sanders of Wessagusset sent a message to Bradford asking him if it would be all right to just plain take the corn by force.

Bradford's answer was: absolutely not! He warned that stealing would ruin all relations with the American Indians from that point on. Unfortunately, word had gotten out to the Massachuset Indians about Sanders's plan. Soon afterward, many nearby tribes had heard the story and agreed to cooperate to wipe out Weston's colony.

Still, Governor Bradford refused to help the undisciplined men of Wessagusset. He pointed out that famine was approaching in Plymouth also, but that oysters, clams, and mussels were still to be found, as well as nuts from the ground. The sixty strong men of Wessagusset could just go ahead and learn about the woods to fill their needs, as the Pilgrims were doing. The best Bradford could do was to offer a few supplies to Sanders so that several men could travel by shallop to Monhegan Island to find more food.

There were two events that changed Bradford's mind. One was that Miles Standish, on a trading trip to the Manomet Indians, confirmed rumors of the combined tribes' wish to rid themselves of the English. The other was that word came to Plymouth of the death of Massasoit, the sachem who had long been the friend and supporter of the Pilgrims. Edward Winslow was sent as the representative to pay his respects to Massasoit. He was accompanied by Hobomok. Winslow brought along a supply of medicine, just in case the rumor of Massasoit's death was wrong.

Massasoit's Sickness

When Winslow arrived at Massasoit's large lodge, he found it very crowded. Medicine men were chanting loudly. Women knelt by Massasoit's mat, rubbing his arms and legs. He was alive, but barely. Massasoit whispered, "*Matta neen wonckanet namen*, Winslow," meaning "I shall never see you again, Winslow."[6]

The old sachem was very sick but was able to swallow the medicine and drink a little water with herbs. Soon he could eat. One more scare came about when

Edward Winslow's wife died during the first winter in the New World. However, he eventually remarried and became the colony's ambassador to the American Indians and the Merchant Adventurers. Winslow would also serve three terms as governor of the Plymouth colony.

he ate too much too soon and nearly died. However, Massasoit recovered and told Winslow that he had been approached to join in a planned attack on Plymouth that would happen at the same time other tribes attacked Wessagusset. Massasoit said he had refused and also had forbidden his people to have any part in the attack.

An Assassination Is Planned

Winslow traveled back to Plymouth as fast as he could. He and Hobomok urged Bradford to kill some Massachuset Indian leaders before they could complete the plans for attack. The problem was brought before public court, and it was decided that Bradford; Allerton, the deputy governor; and Standish must make the final decision.

The three leaders acted swiftly. Standish was to take eight men (which seems incredible since the Massachuset Indians alone had five thousand braves) and go to Wessagusset. Standish was to represent this trip, with its small number of men, as a trip to trade for food. First, they had to be absolutely sure that Plymouth was really about to be attacked. Once they were sure, they were to kill Wituwamat, a powerful sachem of the Massachuset. Standish was sure Wituwamat was the principal leader of the attack plot.

Standish, though a very small man, had endless courage—and a very bad temper. He was a soldier, and in keeping with the ruthless warfare of the time, he planned to behead the sachem and put his head on a pole as a warning to other possible attackers.

Death to Wituwamat!

Indeed, Standish found Wessagusset in worse shape than the Pilgrims could have imagined. The Wessagusset settlers, having treated the American Indians terribly, had caused the Indians to turn against them. All but a few of the leaders, hiding somewhere in the village, had traded even their clothes for food. Now they were living in the woods or being fed like dogs at American Indian villages. Bands of American

Miles Standish's Pilgrim army wore this type of armor to protect themselves from American Indian arrows.

Indians roamed around the former colony, going into and out of the houses. They openly threatened Standish and the eight Pilgrim soldiers. Standish knew he had to make a show of force or the large combined forces of many tribes would ruin Plymouth.

Wituwamat, another sachem named Pecksuot, and two other American Indians were in the habit of visiting one particular house. Standish and four soldiers entered the house without being noticed, and when the Indians arrived, three were killed immediately. The other was hanged outside so that the other Indians loitering around the village would be horrified.

Horrified, they were. The men ran from the village, leaving women and children behind. Standish took the women captive. He sent one of them to tell the braves that Standish would kill the other women if the braves took word of the recent killings to Obtakeist, head sachem of the Massachuset. Eventually the women were released, and as the Wessagusset settlers came back from the woods, Standish refused to let any of them harm or steal from the American Indian women.

Despite the great service that Standish had done for the remaining Wessagusset settlers—all men—most of them ran off to beg favors and food from Obtakeist by telling him of the killings. Standish and his men left Wessagusset for Plymouth. Hobomok, a sachem himself, insisted the American Indians let Standish pass.[7]

Carrying the severed head of Wituwamat, Standish returned to Plymouth. He and eight men had saved the struggling colony from being wiped out. Word spread among the New England tribes that the English God was so strong that nothing they could do would ever make them safe. Says historian H. Roger King,

> The suddenness of the assault on the Massachusetts Indians, and the fear that Standish would move against them next caused the Indians of the Cape to become so terrified that they abandoned their homes for the swamps and deserted areas of the Cape. As a result they became susceptible to contagious disease. A large number of them became ill, and many of them died.[8]

The downward spiral of disease and despair had begun for the New England Indians.

8

HUNGER, TREACHERY, AND PIRATES

The threat of deadly American Indian attack gone by, an equal threat remained in the form of hunger. Not since the first spring of 1621 had the storehouses been so empty.

Here it was, the spring of 1623, and nothing but corn and wheat was still left to be used as seed for planting. There was no news of a ship arriving from England filled with supplies. That first, desperate winter and spring of 1621, almost everyone who had not died of disease worked together to build houses and forts, sharing what little food was available. Two years later, enough time had gone by so that certain individuals and families had become stronger and more capable, working very hard. Others had not followed their example.

A New System of Farming

Plymouth was based on a communal system. Though houses were individual property, the crops were raised for all to share. The families who worked very hard became angry at those who did little work. The hard-working families often felt that the people who did not share in the work should not receive the same amount of corn as those who worked hard.

"Bradford and the members of his council were quickly alive to the changing spirit and acted determinedly to protect the industrious majority from the idle minority," according to historian Vernon Heaton.[1] Bradford did away with the communal system and created a new system. Each family or individual was given one acre of land that was theirs alone to plant, care for, and harvest. Lots would be drawn—and each year the acres were redistributed. This was decided because some acres of land just naturally produced more corn than others.

Since the corn they grew was to be the *only* corn made available to them, it was up to each family to make that a large or small amount. Individuals who held certain necessary jobs that benefited everyone, such as doctors, would be subsidized. That is, each family would have to give a little corn to support those who had a reason to plant less, like doctors. All the settlers were reminded that working on buildings and defenses was to be shared equally, as well as working toward sending back goods to pay off the debt to the Merchant Adventurers.

Governor Bradford noted that this distribution of private land "had very good success; for it made all hands very industrious, so as much more corn was planted than otherwise would have been by any means the Governor or any other could use, and saved him a great deal of trouble, and gave far better

Each pilgrim family had their own garden plots.

content."[2] He goes on to say that even women who had before said they were too weak to work in the field now worked willingly, taking their children with them.

Drought

The new spirit of independence over growing food encouraged people to work harder at other jobs as well. The weather was good. The corn was all planted by the end of April, and hopes that a supply ship would arrive were higher. However, by the beginning of June 1623, the beautiful spring weather turned into a drought. For a month and a half there was little rain, just at the time when young plants most need water as well as sunlight.

In the middle of this terrible blow, a shipwreck was discovered on a nearby coast. This was thought to be the supply ship from England, all supplies now sunk to the bottom of the ocean along with the Pilgrims' hopes. Was God angry with the Pilgrims? It was decided to declare a day of prayer, as Governor Bradford put it, "to humble themselves together before the Lord . . ."[3]

On July 16, the entire colony was to stop work and spend eight hours praying. It was once again a beautiful, cloudless day, but very hot. After the day of prayer, there were a few clouds in the sky. By morning, rain was falling in a soft, constant way that went far to restoring the ailing crops. Though still hungry, the Pilgrims had hope again.

Not only had the drought hurt the Pilgrims, but all the American Indians in the area had also watched their crops fail. Hobomok told his American Indian friends that the new rain was just another example of the strength of the English God—for usually when rain came after a drought it was so heavy that it destroyed the crops. Hobomok felt that because of the prayers of the Pilgrims, there were not even damaging storms—just good, steady rain.

The *Anne* and the *Little James*

Though hopes were high, there was still hunger and no supply ship in view. Miles Standish brought a Scotsman named David Tomson to Plymouth when he returned from a trip to trade with the American Indians. Tomson told of a ship called the *Paragon* that had been sent from England by John Peirce of the Merchant Adventurers in the fall of 1622. The ship was carrying supplies and new settlers. Bad weather forced the ship back to England. It sailed a second time, only to once again barely make it through weeks of storms before sailing back to England. Peirce did not send a new ship. Instead, he resigned his patent and left the company. Other directors had looked for a sturdy ship, and Tomson claimed that one was on its way.

Indeed, a large ship named the *Anne* arrived later that August of 1623, and several days afterward a smaller ship, called a pinnace, the *Little James*, followed. The *Little James* was supposed to stay at Plymouth for use in trading.

The very good news aboard the *Anne* was the arrival of about sixty members of the Separatist congregations at Leyden and London. Family members who had been left behind in 1620 were among the arrivals. Several members of the Brewster family, the wife and children of Francis Cooke and Richard Warren, and the wives of four other men arrived on the *Anne*. Two widows who sailed on the ship would become the wives of Governor Bradford and Miles Standish.

Not all of the new Pilgrims were happy with what they saw. Their former friends from Leyden were practically dressed in rags, their faces were thin and drawn, and they lived in log houses! Their eating habits had changed greatly—there was no beer or ale, no bread, just water and fish!

Some of the new settlers—no exact number is available—had made separate financial arrangements with the Merchant Adventurers. They owed no allegiance to the community and did not have to be part of the general welfare if they chose not to. John Oldham was the leader of this group.

One of the signs of trouble to come was that John Robinson, the pastor of the Leyden Congregation, was not one of the new settlers. The Merchant Adventurers never really believed in the Pilgrims' wish for freedom to worship exactly as they chose. The Pilgrims had opened up the possibility of settling New England, and now it was time to reform the reformers. The need for this colony to finally become profitable for the investors was all-important to the Merchant Adventurers. They did not want to be identified with bringing a nonconformist pastor to the Pilgrims, one who would only increase the Separatists' independence. Too much was at stake.

A New Patent

When the *Anne* left to return to England in September 1623, Edward Winslow went with the ship. This ambassador to the American Indians was also chosen to be the ambassador to the Merchant Adventurers and anyone else in England who might be interested in this new colony. Winslow painted a rosy picture of the possibilities in the New World. This was not of much help to the Pilgrims, however, because all kinds of new seekers of fortune wanted to apply for their own patents for land and settlement.

Finally, Plymouth was granted its own patent. They now held a patent for the actual land they had settled, though they were still in debt to the Merchant Adventurers. Edward Winslow and Robert Cushman held the patent for the Pilgrims. Cushman planned to send a carpenter, a salt maker, and a preacher.

Troublemakers

When Winslow arrived in Plymouth in March 1624, he brought many supplies, and the first livestock—three cows and one bull—to live in Plymouth. However, it was not John Robinson who disembarked the *Anne*, but John Lyford. This man was to become the Pilgrims' official pastor.

The Pilgrims welcomed, with reservations, this new preacher. John Lyford was a Church of England clergyman with Puritan sympathies. Though Lyford pretended to have great reverence and loyalty to the Separatist cause, it soon became clear that he had been sent for the express purpose of undermining the Separatist beliefs. While professing great allegiance to the Separatist church, Lyford began making friends of the "particulars," a term used to describe the non-Separatists led by John Oldham. Lots of talking behind backs, attempts to split the congregation, and writing of letters occurred, to the point where Bradford decided to step in.

Appalling Letters

When the *Anne* was ready to return to England with letters from settlers, Bradford boarded the ship. He told Captain William Pierce that he must give him all letters entrusted to him by John Lyford and John Oldham.

This done, the letters "were found to contain whole series of lying accusations, some of them so seriously prejudicial to the well-being of the settlement and its elected officers that they could not be allowed to pass unchallenged," according to historian Vernon Heaton.[4] Included in the dispatches from the two troublemakers were stolen copies of letters between Robinson and Deacon Brewster and Winslow—commented on with lies in the margins. Oldham completely did himself in by admitting in a letter that Lyford planned to immediately reform the Separatist church and to restore the Church of England rituals!

Bradford left the *Anne* with his pockets full of these letters. Miles Standish was sent to bring Oldham before the governor. Before Standish could accompany Oldham to the governor's chambers, Oldham pulled out a knife, swore at Standish, and told him he had no right to tell him what the governor wanted. Oldham told Bradford much the same thing, and was "clapped up (imprisoned) a while."[5]

Oldham calmed down and was released. Bradford had never revealed anything about the letters. Unbelievably, Lyford and Oldham called a church meeting apart from the usual worship, never bothering to ask or even inform the Pilgrim church elders of this.

Oldham and Lyford Are Banished

Bradford held a court, calling for all in the colony to attend. Lyford and Oldham were charged with secretly plotting and disobeying the accepted order of the colony. The two letter-writers denied the charges. They were then charged with trying to take away the liberty of conscience—the whole reason the Separatist Pilgrims emigrated—by reintroducing the old, ritualistic religion.

Bradford likened what both Lyford and Oldham had done to the old fable of the hedgehog whom the rabbit had let into her burrow during a storm. The hedgehog decided not to leave, and hurt the poor rabbit with her sharp prickers, forcing the generous rabbit to abandon her home to the selfish hedgehog.[6]

Lyford demanded proof. The letters were produced. Lyford grew very silent. Oldham lost his

---

SOURCE DOCUMENT

... ALL THE WORLD KNEW THEY [THE PILGRIMS] CAME ... TO ENJOY THE LIBERTY OF THEIR CONSCIENCE AND THE FREE USE OF GOD'S ORDINANCES, AND FOR THAT END HAD VENTURED THEIR LIVES AND PASSED THROUGH SO MUCH HARDSHIP ... AND THEY AND THEIR FRIENDS HAD BORNE [SIC] THE CHARGE OF THESE BEGINNINGS, WHICH WAS NOT SMALL. ... AND FOR HIM [LYFORD] TO PLOT AGAINST THEM, AND SEEK THEIR RUIN, WAS MOST UNJUST AND PERFIDIOUS [DISLOYAL].[7]

Bradford described the effect that Lyford's betrayal had on the Pilgrims.

temper. Governor Bradford then had every one of the letters read out loud in the council room.

Both men were ordered to leave the colony at once. Oldham's wife and family could stay the winter until he could find a safe place for them. Lyford was given six months to leave—which proved to be a mistake. He continued to write letters to England, somehow smuggling them out. He then left Plymouth, going to Jamestown, Virginia, where he died. Oldham returned to Plymouth once more, in 1625. He once again caused trouble and lost his temper. Again he was imprisoned and then expelled.

More Bad News

This obvious treachery actually had a good effect on the colonists at Plymouth. Most of the people who had arrived with Oldham left as the Pilgrims once again banded together to work for the good of all. The harvest of 1625 was a good one. There was not only enough corn to eat and save until the next harvest, but they had corn to trade with the American Indians. The *Little James* was sent to England filled with furs, and hopes were that the profits from this cargo would finish paying off the debt to the Merchant Adventurers.

Once again, this was not to be. Captain Miles Standish, who had sailed on a larger ship at the same time as the *James*, brought terrible news back with him. The seas were calm and the ship made very good time. However, Barbary pirates from coastal Spain captured the *Little James*, its cargo, and all the crew just as they were about to see land. Captain and crew were sold into slavery in Turkey and never heard from again. The pirates were the only ones who profited from all the Pilgrims' hard work.

This was not the only bad news. Pastor John Robinson had died in Leyden on March 1, 1625, never having reached Plymouth. A terrible plague in England, which had killed forty thousand people, also took Robert Cushman, deacon and advocate of the Pilgrims' cause.

Standish's mission was to talk to Sir Ferdinando Gorges, the powerful colonizer with the Council for New England. The Pilgrims hoped Gorges would help them finally get out from under the unfair practices of the Merchant Adventurers. Gorges refused to help, and now the valuable furs had been pirated at sea. What were the Pilgrims to do?

While all the dramatic, life-threatening events were going on in the new colony of Plymouth, daily life also went on. People were married, children were born, farmwork was done, meals were eaten, houses were cleaned, and parents played with and disciplined their children. The children found time to have fun, but life in seventeenth-century New England was very different from today.

DAILY LIFE AT PLYMOUTH

Holy Days

Of course, we know there was no electricity or running water, no phones or computers. How did people live? What did people do? Mostly, they worked, especially in this new colony where everything had to be built from scratch and food was short. The Pilgrims worked all the time, stopping on Saturday afternoon and beginning again on Monday morning. This break from work, however, was not a holiday filled with celebration. This was the Sabbath—very important to the religious Pilgrims. On this day, they read the Bible to

Most pictures of the Pilgrims are of them in their church clothes. These pilgrims are on their way to church. Men with guns guard the other churchgoers, keeping a watchful eye on the woods.

themselves or to their children, and games and loud play were not allowed.

Sunday was spent in the meetinghouse, often for many hours. Children sat on hard wooden benches and were watched over by deacons. Hymns were sung and the ruling elder or minister delivered a lengthy sermon.

Corn-watchers and Spit Turners

When the workday approached, boys and girls worked alongside their parents. Boys were corn-watchers. They sat on a stand above the cornfield and

Pilgrim boys would watch the corn from a wooden tower. If a bird came near, the boys would scare it away.

threw rocks or sticks at crows and other birds that would have liked to make a meal of the Pilgrims' corn. When the corn was ready, both boys and girls scraped it off the cobs, either against the edge of a shovel or a long pan handle.

If a turkey was to be cooked, which took about seven hours over the hearth fire, boys and girls worked the iron spit—a long rod. This rod held the turkey over the fire and was turned so that the large bird could cook evenly. Children also gathered grasses for making thatched roofs, picked up mussels from the rocks, and dug for clams in the sand. They picked berries and collected nuts. They stuffed linen bags with corncobs, pine needles, or feathers to make mattresses.

The girls helped out in the house, with the washing, cooking, and serving. Boys helped build, especially making wooden pegs for hanging clothes and cookware. In between all this work, girls played with homemade dolls, and boys played jumping and running games and learned to shoot a gun.

Daily Wear

In illustrations of Pilgrims they all seem to be dressed alike—the men in black with stiff hats, the women in gray with white aprons and collars and white linen caps. However, those were their Sunday clothes. During the week they wore bright colors. The women wore long woolen dresses in red, green, or blue with white linen caps and red or purple capes. The men wore long-sleeved woolen or leather jackets called doublets and pants called breeches. They had long stockings of red or green wool and knitted stocking caps. Boys were dressed in long dresses until they were six!

Where They Lived

The Pilgrim houses were small, with no glass in the windows and steep roofs covered with thatch. There was a big room shared by everyone, sometimes with a loft above. A bed in those days meant a mattress, sometimes on a raised board. If they were lucky, the mattress was filled with feathers. The children slept in trundle beds that pushed underneath their parents' bed during the day, or slept in the loft if they were over seven.

Dinner was served on wooden boards across two wooden sawhorses. These were moved at night so the mattresses could be put on the floor. On one side of the room was a fireplace where all the cooking and heating and lighting of the room went on. Clothes, as well as guns and helmets, were hung on pegs on the wall. A pine chest held Sunday clothes, sheets, and blankets.

Eaten Plates and Dirty Napkins

During dinner the children were not to speak unless a grown-up spoke first, and they stood by the table with their hats on. Pilgrims ate with their fingers, the occasional wooden spoon, or clamshells. Knives were the same as those used for hunting. For plates the Pilgrims used either a trencher, which was a piece of wood scooped out on one side, or a piece of stale bread.

The best Pilgrim beds were filled with feathers, like this one inside a present-day reconstruction of a Pilgrim house.

Referring to the bread, historian Lucille Recht Penner says, "It wasn't hard to clean up after a Pilgrim meal. Especially if you ate the plates."[1] A whole pot of food, almost always with corn somewhere in it, was put on the table, and everyone, except small children who ate what their parents handed to them, dipped into the pot with fingers or knife. They used big napkins, hung around their necks. Cups made of gourds or wood were dipped into a big barrel of water. At the end of a meal, a voider—a big basket—was passed around and the trenchers, spoons, and cups went into it.[2]

The dirty napkins were put away and would be used again. Linens and clothes were washed only twice a year. Soap had to be made from ashes and animal fat, and water, taken from the stream, was heated in big pots.

Education

The first year at Plymouth there was no school, and children learned at home by means of hornbooks— pieces of wood covered with a paper on which the alphabet was written. These were covered with a thin sheet of animal horn—so thin one could see through it to the letters beneath. There were no storybooks; children read only the Bible.

Strict Laws

There was much monitoring of daily life in Plymouth. It was a crime to play on a Sunday, a crime to get drunk or engage in any "wild" behavior, and, of course, it was a crime to steal. Punishments included

The Pilgrims used many different types of vessels to prepare and serve food.

being whipped in public or being branded with a red-hot iron. One could also be set in the stocks—two wooden parts with holes in the middle for head and arms that were snapped together when a person was fitted through them. A person could be fined, and for terrible crimes, hung. All this was a strong incentive to "provide an image of the ideal that those in authority strove to achieve for society," write historians James Deetz and Patricia Scott Deetz.[3]

As food became more plentiful and other colonists arrived and formed new settlements, there would be more variety in food and clothing, and the houses would become bigger and better furnished. But for the first four years of this struggling colony, simpler was better, and order within society was necessary.

10

EXPANSION AND LEGACY

Four years after the Plymouth Colony had come into being, there were only 108 people and 32 houses. And still, no matter how many ships full of furs and other valuable cargo the Pilgrims shipped, they seemed never to be able to pay off the debt to the Merchant Adventurers. Efforts to end the debt had met with piracy, shipwreck, change of monetary value, and treachery. Each time the colony believed its debt was paid, it was informed that it still owed. In order to wipe out the debt and put Plymouth on a sound financial basis, the colony needed to expand. More beaver and other fur must be sent to England to pay off the debt. Trade with the valuable American Indians was increased, and there was never again to be a full-scale threat of famine.

More Colonies

However, as the years went on, other colonies were beginning on land the Pilgrims had thought was theirs. King James had died and King Charles I replaced him. Charles was even more anti-Puritan and

As the Plymouth colony became more successful, the settlers were able to grow and cook types of food that were not available when they were struggling. Though their wheat crop failed the first few winters, they were later able to make bread. All of the Pilgrims were allowed to use the communal bread oven.

anti-Separatist than James had been. Many Puritans fled England and started towns on Massachusetts Bay, including Salem and Boston.

The self-contained little colony of Plymouth became more involved in setting up beaver-trading posts around New England, in competition with other

Puritan colonies. The Pilgrims engaged in ever-wider trade with American Indians and with other European settlers. This trade extended as far north as present-day Maine and as far south as Manhattan Island. By 1627, properties were divided between families and single men in an extension of the 1623 allotment of specific farming plots for each family. The Pilgrim communal system ceased to grow.

By the 1630s, Pilgrim settlers began to spread out into other colonies. In the meantime, Puritans had begun to emigrate in much larger quantity than the early Pilgrim Separatists. Many of the Puritans were educated people of wealth, rank, and education. They were fleeing the persecution of Charles I, who was more effective in his punishments than James I.

In 1630, nine hundred Puritans left England in eleven ships, carrying with them livestock, supplies, and no debt. Though these settlers also endured the hardships of winter and unfamiliar food and living conditions, they had more resources—and people—at their disposal than the Pilgrims had in 1620. In addition, the Pilgrims had already dealt with relations among the American Indian population. The Puritans' settlements were prospering colonies within a year of the settlers' arrival in the New World.

The settlement at Duxbury was begun in 1632, on land containing lots owned by none other than Miles Standish. Other towns begun by outreach from Plymouth were Scituate, Taunton, Sandwich, Barnstable, Yarmouth, and Marshfield. Plymouth

John Winthrop led the Puritan settlers to Massachusetts Bay in 1630, and became governor of the colony.

itself became the county seat of Massachusetts Bay Colony in 1633.

The Ongoing Debt

By 1635, the Pilgrims were still trying to pay off the debt. Beaver, otter, mink, and fox pelts weighing 3,678 pounds were sent to London. This time the ship arrived. Still, it was not enough.

By 1643, four colonies of Massachusetts consisting of the original Pilgrims and the Puritans became "The United Colonies of New England." These active colonies were Plymouth, Connecticut, Rhode Island, and New Haven.

One of the traits that both helped and hindered the Pilgrims was that they were honorable people. They preferred to continue to try to meet their obligations rather than confront the dishonest element in fellow

Though most historians no longer believe that the Pilgrims landed at Plymouth Rock, the rock has come to symbolize the perseverance of America's early European settlers. To honor Plymouth Rock, a monument has been erected around it.

human beings. They finally met their ongoing debt after twenty-eight years. In 1648, several prominent citizens sold their own houses and farms, gathering the final four hundred pounds.

The Pilgrim's Legacy

Plymouth actually was absorbed by Massachusetts in 1692. It was many years later that the Pilgrims were recognized as the founders of New England. Freedom of religion, trial by jury of twelve men, the town meeting—all these were the way of the Pilgrims.

This small group of independent people proved that initiative based on belief, not just rules, counts. These immigrants to a new land used their own and the land's resources to build a home and a life for themselves. They encountered many dangers along the way, including death. The Pilgrims freed themselves of the censorship of their beliefs that had caused them to emigrate in the first place. They lived, and prospered, and their descendents went on to found a nation built at least in part on the early principles of the Mayflower Compact.

When Plymouth became part of the royal province of Massachusetts, this was not a loss—but a continuance. The Pilgrims were not always tolerant of others' beliefs, though they sought tolerance for their own. They were also totally naïve about what they would encounter in a new land. However, many of the Pilgrims' ideals are now American ideals: liberty, democracy, and freedom of religion and politics.

The Founding Fathers started the United States by insisting on freedom. While Americans no longer live as the Pilgrims did, or face the same dangers and discomforts, they have the Pilgrims to thank for believing so strongly in the freedoms that are taken for granted every day. Theirs is a story of strength, honesty, and survival, which gave rise to the very spirit of America's democracy.

★ TIMELINE ★

1606—A group of Separatists from Gainsborough, England, begins meeting in Scrooby.

1608—Scrooby Separatists move to Amsterdam, Holland.

1609—Some of the Scrooby Separatists move from Amsterdam to Leyden, Holland.

1614—John Smith completes a map of New England.

1616—John Smith's book *A Description of New England* is published.

1620—*July 21*: Separatist Pilgrims leave Leyden.

September 6: The *Mayflower* sets sail from Plymouth, England, with funding from the Merchant Adventurers.

November 9: Land sighted from the *Mayflower*.

November 11: Mayflower Compact signed; John Carver elected first governor of Plymouth colony; Pilgrims first set foot on land in New England.

December 8: Pilgrims have their first armed encounter with American Indians.

December 11: A Pilgrim exploring party lands at Plymouth Harbor. (Legend says they landed at Plymouth Rock, but most historians disagree with this.)

December 20: Site picked for Plymouth colony.

December 25: Pilgrims begin building houses.

1621—*March 16*: Pilgrims meet Samoset.

March 22–23: Pilgrims meet Squanto and Massasoit; Pilgrims sign treaty with Wampanoag.

March 31: Almost half of the original 102 Pilgrims have died.

April 5: William Bradford elected governor after John Carver dies.

May 12: First marriage in Plymouth occurs between Edward Winslow and Susanna White.

Fall: Pilgrims' first harvest is a good one.

October: First Thanksgiving Day is held between the Pilgrims and the Wampanoag.

November 11: The *Fortune* arrives with thirty-five new settlers.

December: The *Fortune* leaves with goods for the Merchant Adventurers, but the ship is later robbed by pirates and the payment is never received.

1622—*Mourt's Relation* is published; It is revealed that Squanto has been stirring up trouble among the local American Indian tribes.

June 22: Thomas Weston, formerly of the Merchant Adventurers, sends sixty settlers.

Fall: Wessagusset colony is founded by Thomas Weston's men; Pilgrims have a poor harvest.

December 22: Squanto dies.

1623—Miles Standish and other Pilgrims kill Massachuset Indian leaders in failed Wessagusset colony in effort to discourage an American Indian attack on Plymouth; William Bradford does away with communal system of farming by giving land to each family for private use; Plymouth suffers a drought in June and July; The *Anne* and *Little James* arrive with about sixty more Pilgrims, some of whom are against the Separatist cause; Pilgrims granted patent for the land they settled.

1624—John Lyford and John Oldham are found guilty of plotting against Plymouth colony and are banished.

1625—*Little James* sent to England with payment for Merchant Adventurers, but is robbed by pirates before it reaches its destination.

1633—Plymouth becomes county seat of Massachusetts Bay colony.

1635—Pilgrims send a payment to the Merchant Adventurers.

1643—Plymouth becomes part of the United Colonies of New England.

1648—Pilgrims deliver their final payment to the Merchant Adventurers.

1692—Plymouth is absorbed by the colony of Massachusetts.

★ CHAPTER NOTES ★

Chapter 1. Land Ho!

1. Margaret Wise Brown, ed., *Homes in the Wilderness, A Pilgrim's Journal of Plymouth Plantation in 1620* (Hamden, Conn.: Linnet Books, 1988), p. 1.

2. Ibid.

3. Lucille Recht Penner, *Eating the Plates: A Pilgrim Book of Food and Manners* (New York: Macmillan Publishing Company, 1991), p. 10.

Chapter 2. In Search of Religious Freedom

1. Frank G. Beardsley, *The Builders of a Nation* (Boston: The Gorham Press, 1921), p. 59.

2. James Deetz and Patricia Scott Deetz, *The Times of Their Lives* (New York: W.H. Freeman and Company, 2000), p. 32.

Chapter 3. The First Emigration

1. William Bradford, *Of Plymouth Plantation 1620–1647* (New York: Alfred A. Knopf, 1997), p. 11.

2. Ibid., p. 12.

3. Ibid., p. 13.

4. Ibid., p. 14.

5. Ibid.

6. Ibid., pp. 14–15.

7. James Deetz and Patricia Scott Deetz, *The Times of Their Lives* (New York: W.H. Freeman and Company, 2000), p. 35.

Chapter 4. Setting Out for America

1. James Deetz and Patricia Scott Deetz, *The Times of Their Lives* (New York: W.H. Freeman and Company, 2000), p. 35.

2. William Bradford, *Of Plymouth Plantation 1620–1647* (New York: Alfred A. Knopf, 1997), p. 59.

3. Deetz and Deetz, p. 39.

Chapter 5. The Mayflower Compact

1. James Deetz and Patricia Scott Deetz, *The Times of Their Lives* (New York: W.H. Freeman and Company, 2000), p. 19.

2. Ibid., p. 20.

3. Ibid.

4. Margaret Wise Brown, ed., *Homes in the Wilderness, A Pilgrim's Journal of Plymouth Plantation in 1620* (Hamden, Conn.: Linnet Books, 1988), p. 24.

5. H. Roger King, *Cape Cod and Plymouth Colony in the Seventeenth Century* (Lanham, Md.: University Press of America, Inc., 1994), p. 20.

6. Brown, p. 37.

7. Ibid., p. 37–38.

8. Deetz and Deetz, p. 18.

9. George F. Willison, *Saints and Strangers* (Orleans, Miss.: Parnassus Imprints, Inc., 1993), p. 156.

10. Ibid., pp. 156–157.

Chapter 6. The Howling of Wolves

1. Margaret Wise Brown, ed., *Homes in the Wilderness, A Pilgrim's Journal of Plymouth Plantation*

in 1620 (Hamden, Conn.: Linnet Books, 1988), p. 54.

2. Ibid., p. 58.

3. Ibid., p. 64.

4. Ibid.

5. Feenie Ziner, *The Pilgrims and Plymouth Colony* (New York: American Heritage Publishing Co., 1961), p. 96.

6. Brown, p. 69.

7. Vernon Heaton, *The Mayflower* (Exeter, England: Webb and Bower Limited, 1980), p. 138.

Chapter 7. Betrayal and the Threat of War

1. Vernon Heaton, *The Mayflower* (Exeter, England: Webb and Bower Limited, 1980), p. 154.

2. James Deetz and Patricia Scott Deetz, *The Times of Their Lives* (New York: W.H. Freeman and Company, 2000), p. 64.

3. William Bradford, *Of Plymouth Plantation 1620–1647* (New York: Alfred A. Knopf, 1997), p. 80.

4. Heaton, p. 158.

5. Frank G. Beardsley, *The Builders of a Nation* (Boston: The Gorham Press, 1921), p. 191.

6. Heaton, pp. 179–180.

7. H. Roger King, *Cape Cod and Plymouth Colony in the Seventeenth Century* (Lanham, Md.: University Press of America, Inc., 1994), p. 29.

8. King, p. 29.

Chapter 8. Hunger, Treachery, and Pirates

1. Vernon Heaton, *The Mayflower* (Exeter, England: Webb and Bower Limited, 1980), p. 182.

2. Frank G. Beardsley, *The Builders of a Nation* (Boston: The Gorham Press, 1921), p. 265.

3. William Bradford, *Of Plymouth Plantation 1620–1647* (New York: Alfred A. Knopf, 1997), p. 131.

4. Heaton, pp. 185–186.

5. Bradford, p. 151.

6. Ibid., p. 152.

7. Ibid., pp. 151–152.

Chapter 9. Daily Life at Plymouth

1. Lucille Recht Penner, *Eating the Plates: A Pilgrim Book of Food and Manners* (New York: Macmillan Publishing Company, 1991), p. 83.

2. Ibid., pp. 76–77, 80, 84.

3. James Deetz and Patricia Scott Deetz, *The Times of Their Lives* (New York: W.H. Freeman and Company, 2000), p. 133.

★ Further Reading ★

Brown, Margaret Wise, ed. *Homes in the Wilderness: A Pilgrim's Journal of Plymouth Plantation in 1620, by William Bradford and Others of the Mayflower Company.* North Haven, Conn.: Shoe String Press, Inc., 1988.

Dubowski, Cathy East. *The Story of Squanto: First Friend to the Pilgrims.* Milwaukee: Gareth Stevens, Inc., 1997.

Erickson, Paul. *Daily Life in the Pilgrim Colony 1636.* New York: Houghton Mifflin Company, 2001.

Hale, Anna W. *The Mayflower People: Triumphs and Tragedies.* Boulder, Colo.: Roberts Rinehart Publishers, 1995.

Miller, Susan Martins. *Miles Standish.* Broomall, Pa.: Chelsea House Publishers, 1999.

Stein, R. Conrad. *The Pilgrims.* Danbury, Conn.: Children's Press, 1995.

Whitehurst, Susan. *The First Thanksgiving.* New York: The Rosen Publishing Group, Inc., 2002.

———. *The Mayflower: Pilgrims Before the Mayflower.* New York: The Rosen Publishing Group, Inc., 2002.

———. *Plymouth: Surviving the First Winter.* New York: The Rosen Publishing Group, Inc., 2002.

★ Internet Addresses ★

"America's Museum of Pilgrim Possessions." *Pilgrim Hall Museum*. n.d. <http://www.pilgrimhall.org/>.

Plimoth-on-Web. November 15, 2001. <http://www.plimoth.org/>.

"Plymouth, Mass." *America's Homepage!* © 1995–1999. <http://pilgrims.net/plymouth/>.

★ INDEX ★

A

Alden, John, 37, 82, 83
Allerton, Isaac, 64, 86
Anne, 94, 95, 96, 97

B

Bradford, William, 17, 22,
  25, 26, 35, 39, 46, 49,
  51, 52, 56, 61, 64, 72,
  73, 74, 76, 77, 79, 83,
  84, 86, 91, 96, 97,
  98, 99
Brewster, William, 15, 16,
  17, 20, 23, 27, 28, 29,
  31, 35, 38, 56, 70, 97
Browne, Peter, 55
Browne, Robert, 14, 15, 16
Butten, William, 40

C

Calvin, John, 12
Canonicus, 73
Carver, John, 31, 43, 49,
  62, 64
Charles I, king of England,
  110, 112
Church of England, 14, 17,
  19, 20, 21, 25, 27, 38,
  96, 97
Clyfton, Richard, 22, 23, 26
Common House, 53, 57
Cooke, Francis, 56, 94
Corn Hill, 47
*The Courtship of Miles
  Standish*, 82
Cushman, Robert, 31, 38,
  70–71, 72, 96, 100

D

*A Description of New
  England*, 29

E

Edward VI, king of
  England, 13
Elizabeth, queen of England,
  14, 16, 18

F

Fort Hill, 53, 54, 57, 74
Fortune, 70, 71, 72, 81

G

Goodman, John, 55
Gorges, Ferdinando, 33, 34,
  61, 71, 100
Greenwood, John, 16, 17

H

Henry VIII, king of
  England, 13
Hobomok, 74, 76, 80, 84,
  86, 88, 93
Hopkins, Stephen, 39, 54,
  59, 65, 66, 73

J

James I, king of England,
  18, 19, 20, 23, 28, 29,
  31, 43, 110, 111, 112
Jamestown, Virginia, 9, 29,
  31, 34, 82, 99
Jones, Christopher, 41,
  47, 57

L

Little James, 94, 99

Longfellow, Henry
Wadsworth, 82
Luther, Martin, 12
Lyford, John, 96, 97, 98, 99

M
Manomet Indians, 84
Mary, queen of England,
13–14
Massachuset Indians, 73,
74, 81, 83, 86, 88
Massasoit, 59, 61, 62, 64,
66, 68, 69, 76, 77, 79,
80, 84, 86
Mayflower, 7, 9, 10, 11,
35, 36, 37, 38, 39, 41,
53, 64
Mayflower Compact, 42,
43, 45, 52, 115
Merchant Adventurers, 9,
32, 33, 34, 59–60, 71,
80, 81, 91, 94, 95, 96,
99, 100, 110
Mourt's Relation, 7, 49, 59,
62, 72
Mullens, Priscilla, 82, 83

N
Narragansett Indians, 62,
63, 72, 73, 74, 76
Nauset Indians, 60

O
Obtakeist, 88
Of Plymouth Plantation, 22
Oldham, John, 95, 96, 97,
98, 99

P
Paragon, 94
Paspahegh Indians, 82
Patuxet Indians, 60, 61

Pecksuot, 88
Penry, John, 16, 17
Philip II, king of Spain, 13
Pilgrims
daily life, 101–102,
104–105, 107, 109
and the first Thanksgiving
Day, 66, 68–69
relationship with the
American Indians, 46,
49, 55, 56, 57, 59–64,
65–66, 68–69, 70,
72–77, 79–80, 83,
84, 86, 87–89, 93,
110, 112
Plymouth, 7, 9, 28, 33, 40,
43, 45, 50, 51, 52, 56,
59, 60, 64, 65, 66, 70,
71, 73, 74, 76, 77, 80,
82, 83, 84, 86, 88, 90,
94, 96, 99, 100, 101,
107, 110, 111, 114, 115

R
Robinson, John, 20, 23, 26,
27, 33, 95, 96, 97, 100

S
Samoset, 57, 59, 60, 64
Sanders, John, 83, 84
Smith, John, 29, 33, 50, 60
Smyth, John, 21
Sowams, 64, 66, 76, 79,
Speedwell, 35, 37, 38
Squanto, 60, 61, 64, 66, 68,
73, 74, 75, 76, 77, 79,
80, 81, 83

Standish, Miles, 37, 43, 46, 49, 53, 54, 56, 57, 60, 61, 62, 72, 74, 76, 81, 82, 83, 84, 86, 87, 88, 89, 93, 94, 97, 99, 100, 112

T

Tomson, David, 94

V

Virginia Company of London, 9, 29, 31

Virginia Company of Plymouth, 9

W

Wampanoag Indians, 59, 61, 62, 63, 64, 66, 68, 73, 76, 77, 79, 80,

Warren, Richard, 94

Waymouth, George, 34, 60

Wessagusset, 81, 82, 83, 84, 86, 87, 88,

Weston, Thomas, 32, 33, 34, 71, 72, 81, 82, 83

White, Susanna, 65

Winslow, Edward, 49, 56, 61, 62, 64, 65, 66, 70, 72, 73, 84, 86, 95, 96, 97

Wituwamat, 86, 88

Wyclif, John, 12